# THE

# CRAYFORD

# STORY

*David McMullan receives his MBE from the Queen in recognition of his work for Oxfam*

# The CRAYFORD Story

by

**David McMullan** MBE

**A success story of specialist car production from the 1960s to 1980s**

ISBN: 978-0-9574108-0-0 hardback

First published in the UK by
Ideal Publications Ltd,
58 Geraint Rd, Downham,
Bromley, Kent BR1 5DX
All enquiries to Barry Priestman at
crayfordclub@hotmail.com



Publishing Consultancy: Zoesbooks: www.zoesbooks.co.uk

Typeset and cover by Helm Information
amandahelm@helm-information.co.uk
www.helm-information.co.uk

Printed and bound in Great Britain by Berforts Group,
Stevenage, Herts SG1 2BH

# Contents

*Barry Priestman, founder of the Crayford Convertible Car Club*

*Austin 3 litre Estate*

# Acknowledgements

Barry Priestman, founder and Chairman of the Crayford Convertible Car Club kindly supplied much of the detailed information and photographs I required for this book .

The Reverend Robin Paterson read and corrected the proof copies, in some cases several times, as I lost track of the content detail over a six-year writing period.

David Harris, a close friend of both the McMullan and Smith families during the early Tatsfield days, has done some valuable checking for me. He enjoys a rare skill: that of a truly literate engineer.

My wife Donna has proved to be an enthusiastic and creative proof-reader. Many of her original ideas have been incorporated into the book. Her steady hand has also been responsible for some of the more recent photographs.

*Main entrance to the Crayford factory, Westerham*

# Preface

This is a personal account of the growth and development of a specialist car conversion business based in the secluded village of Tatsfield, near Westerham, Kent. The two men behind the project, David McMullan and Jeffrey Smith, first teamed up whilst working in the late 1950s at the Lambretta Trojan works, in Croydon, South London. Equipped with nothing more than a toolbox each and the bank's investment of £40, David McMullan set up their fledgling business. Initially they were working from lock-up garages. That was in 1962. The following year they launched the *Crayford* Mini convertible in the national press. At the time it cost £129.00 – around twenty percent uplift on the car price.

*Crayford* – a name that was to become synonymous with top quality specialist car production, both in the UK and abroad – secured a niche position in the motor industry with the registration of *Crayfords Auto Developments Ltd.* in 1966. By then newly-established in its own factory in Westerham, Kent, the company grew steadily into a flourishing and profitable business with a world-wide franchise, producing conversions ranging from Minis to powerful bullet-proof Mercedes – and so much more.

The rise of *Crayford* in the 1960/70s was a phenomena which totally bucked the trend at that period, when the British motor industry was in a state of almost total collapse. Few companies of this type and scale came through these troubled times unscathed, let alone maintained a successful production and sales record. *Crayford* was the exception and the fact that this two-man business not only survived but also flourished was due to a combination of drive and initiative – and the talents of a gifted motor engineer, the late Jeff Smith.

In *The Crayford Story* David McMullan looks back and traces the difficulties and triumphs of the Kent-based company – from its earliest beginnings to its final sale on his retirement in 1987. His account is a warm and often touching story of grit, determination and tireless innovation, all of which combined to lead to their success in a hugely competitive global market.

Keith Nurse

# Chapter 1

# Two Men and a Toolbox

It was a damp, late summer's evening in June 1960. I pulled up my Triumph Thunderbird motorcycle to chat to some of the staff at the Lambretta works on the Kingston by-pass, in Surrey. Casually, I asked if there was someone I could speak to about a job. To my amazement the response was instant. Wet, crumpled and now nervous, I was ushered into a smart office for what turned out to be an impromptu and career-turning interview. Before I knew it, I had landed myself a job in 'Sales', for the Lambretta concessionaires for Great Britain.

On the strength of the new job I moved into a small bedsit on Coombe Hill soon afterwards. It was to be here, in a dingy back room, that my first business was born – and also swiftly died. Trading under the unappealing name of CPAS (Car Purchase Advisory Service), I tapped out letters on a second-hand typewriter, giving advice and recommendations to potential customers. But, as it turned out, there was little interest in what I had to offer – a service effectively made redundant because, as I found to my cost, almost everyone has access to some form of motor expertise already, usually in the form of the legendary friend 'who knows all about cars'. Interestingly, many years later, one of my sons came up with exactly the same advisory service idea, this time working in California, and ran into precisely the same problem.

Then another sideline idea beckoned: car rentals. I tracked down an executive working for a well-known rental firm, eager to pick his brains. Just as well I did the research, because I was quickly deterred by the prospect of the high upfront costs and insurance commitments . It became clear to me that it would be unwise to leave the full-time job at Lambretta until I had carried out more detailed research and could actually get a business up and running. To this day I am not sure why I felt this urge to start and run my own business, but two events I do remember.

My mother told me that when she was a teacher at King's School, Rochester, during the early days of the war she went to see the headmaster and told him she was thinking of starting her own small prep school. She was apprehensive that it might fail: but the headmaster (probably E. W. Davies) replied:

'Mrs. McMullan, you could set the Thames on fire!' and perhaps I inherited her 'self-starter' attitude. My mother never forgot his encouragement.

The other event I remember clearly was walking down the central aisle of the Earls Court London Motor Show in about 1959, when I was Sales Manager of the Elva Sports car division at Lambretta Trojan and deciding that one day I would have my own company stand at the Motor Show … and I did!

But I had to be patient and sound thinking won the moment. There were also other factors to consider, such as the three essentials for success – or the 3Ms, as my economics professor called them: manpower, money and machinery. Subsequently, in the course of my long career as an entrepreneur, I discovered how sound his advice had been.

With his words always ringing in my ears, I finally managed to bring all three imperatives together when I formed my first successful business venture – Burgess Sales. Manpower? Well, that was unquestionably and singularly me. Money?

Yes, it came in the form of £40 I had managed to borrow from Barclays Bank, Bexleyheath. Machinery? Well, the tools at least, were financed by the bank loan. 'Dai the bank', an accommodating and cheery Welshman, was the branch manager and to become a great friend of the family. I can still clearly recall the feeling of trepidation as I first approached him about a 'substantial loan'. I feared he would think me 'off my rocker', wanting to try and start an engineering business with such flimsy resources. Yet he clearly saw my enthusiasm and potential and gave me the loan to buy the all-important tools for the job.

I was not at all happy at the thought of borrowing money from the bank, even though a small amount. Brought up with the strict Ulster attitude of only buying something that you could actually afford to pay for, the idea of purchasing something that I could not really afford went against the grain. Jeffrey felt as I did and we built up the business on that very healthy basis. Even the first car we converted, a used Mini AF0 887 supplied from the family garage in Brecon and available, I am sure, on a 'pay later' basis, was not collected until we had earned all the cash. In later years we were so financially healthy that we often lent surplus funds to Barclays Bank, Westerham, on one-month deposit terms.

At this early stage I was still employed by Lambretta. The company had by then branched out into importing Go-karts – karts to us – from the United States. I had been promoted to Sales Manager and, to borrow an expression from across the Atlantic, was 'driving my butt off' as the No. 1 driver for the company at major racing events across Europe. Kart-racing proved to be a significant development, as from this emerged the opportunity for another sideline venture and one that was to lead to a crucial link-up with Jeff Smith, the man who would become my life-long business partner and friend.

Jeff, a gifted engineer, hailed from Talybont, a village near Brecon. Brought over from South Wales by Ian Williams, chief engineer at Lambretta Trojan, he had been appointed head of Experimental Engineering at the Croydon factory, a role which also put him in charge of race preparation.

As ever, technical innovation was the key to success. We were using solid, non-clutched drive from the engines to link to the rear axle of the karts and needed an automatic clutch system for it to work better. By chance, I discovered that there was a French moped clutch that would do the trick and privately bought one for Jeff and me to experiment with. Then I engaged a firm in Dartford, Kent, to cut off the sprocket and weld on the part I needed for the kart.

The advantage of this innovation was that the engine could be kept running on the starting grid, meaning that it would be hot and ready to fire into action long before the flag dropped. This was quite a breakthrough. I decided to promote it actively, sending out my own leaflets to various RAF camps where I knew from earlier service experience that 'karting' was a major leisure-time activity. There was great excitement when within days the first order arrived at my flat, then at Crayford, near Dartford, Kent. I quickly made the princely sum of £4.00 off the back of the French clutch conversion and soon had a shopping list of kart accessories, which I sent out to various kart-racing clubs. From then on my weekends were mostly spent packing and despatching kart parts.

Not until some time later did I discover that Peter Agg, the managing director at Lambretta, was perfectly aware of my little ventures 'on the side'. But evidently he had concluded that it was causing no harm and, in any event, I was at this time also filling the factory shelves with trophies, having won both the European and the British Manufacturers' Class Two Kart Racing Championships. I had also represented Britain along with Stirling Moss and Roger Biss at the World Championships in Nassau and it was in the Bahamas that I picked up another idea.

The renowned JLO motors came from a specialist engine

factory in Germany, which had been supplying Lambretta Trojan with highly tuned engines. Although our karts were reaching more than 100 mph on the straight at Nassau, some of the rival models from the US were even faster, being equipped with streamlined fibreglass front nose cowlings. I took careful note and brought the idea back with me to England.

Meanwhile Jeff Smith and I had become close friends. As the leading engineer in the Lambretta Experimental Department, he was, for me, a key person, being the man with the vital technical and inventive know-how I knew I would need for future ventures of my own.

During my undergraduate years that led to an Honours B.Sc. with Economics as one of my subjects, I had learned the importance of getting started from the famous quotation from Goethe:

> Whatever you can do, or dream you can do, begin it. Boldness has genius, power and magic in it.

This I typed onto two pieces of card and gave to my sons when they left England to try their luck in California. Twenty-five years later, the quotation seems to have worked. They have both been successful and I think I recently noticed one of the quotation cards still stuck inside a toolbox lid!

To return to Jeff and our kart-racing times, no matter how many decisions, 'nutty' or otherwise, concerning engineering changes and winning tactics came out of the Lambretta Trojan boardroom, at 2.00 pm the following Saturday and Sunday – be it in Germany or elsewhere – everything depended on what Jeff (with the agreement of Ian Williams) had built in 'Experimental' and loaded onto the transporter for shipment to the next kart race. For several years this system worked well, albeit with the occasional hair-raising moments. None more so than in 1961, when quite the worst incident occurred in a kart race at the German circuit in München Gladbach in Germany.

It was Spring 1961 and Jeff had decided to build a chassis with the engine close up alongside the driver, a construction design well ahead of its time, although now universal. However, he decided to drive the kart himself, which spelt disaster. Thirty minutes into the race something terrible happened, but as the other driver in the team I only became aware that something was wrong when I received the signal from the pits to 'press on'. There is, of course, a strong temptation to stop racing when you see a colleague in serious trouble. On the back straight, I swept past Jeff, lying on the ground at the side of the track with race marshals kneeling beside him. He was unconscious and, as I later discovered, suffering from severe head injuries. The RAF flew him back to the UK, but the effects of the crash remained with Jeff for the rest of his life and that image of my friend lying prostrate and immobile as I roared by will remain with me forever.

Yet another alarming incident occurred the same year during the French Grand Prix at the Orly Circuit. Four hours into the race I was in front and going strong, despite the bad weather. I remember our great motoring journalist friend, the late Courtney Edwards, standing in the pouring rain waving at me enthusiastically every time I passed the pits. Then, at the height of the excitement, a problem: the engine on my kart started misfiring, but it was doing so only at full power, on the main straight. On my next refuelling stop, Jeff – who was boss in the pits – concluded that the emergency cut-out wire was earthing, caused by the torrential rain. A moment before accelerating out of the pits, he bent forward and cut the kill switch wire which ran up the steering column with his penknife. It could have worked, but – alas – didn't. As I rejoined the race, the loose wire fell on the chassis, triggering a complete electrical short and engine failure. This was one race which, for us at least, was over in an instant. A bitter, bitter disappointment after several hours of racing, right on the limit.

*David McMullan at the French Grand Prix, Orly 1960*

Inevitably, passions ran high on such occasions, both on and off the circuit. But then we were young (both in our early 30s) and headstrong. Later that evening, fuelled perhaps by the frustrations arising from the bitter race track disappointment earlier, we became involved in an 'after-dinner altercation' with some Parisians.

Ian Williams, a lifelong friend and man of great physical bulk and presence, as well as being chief engineer at Lambretta Trojan, promptly dispensed with all the traditional conventions of the *entente cordiale*, by placing his large boot on the foot of a rather smaller and understandably intimidated Frenchman. Ian, in his own way, simply wanted to hold him still whilst he talked to him. When matters developed in earnest, Roger Biss, a fellow team driver, was seen shooting off in the opposite direction from the fracas. From that day on he became known as 'Sprinter Biss', an accolade which had nothing to do with his famed skills as one of the fastest men on the racing circuits.

We were working in a hugely competitive, demanding and exhilarating environment and with this atmosphere as a backdrop my friendship with chief 'experimental' engineer Jeff Smith developed and blossomed, and in the most unlikely of contexts.

I heard on the grapevine that locally in Kent an order for fertiliser spreaders was on the cards. This was equipment which could be assembled easily on the rear of farm tractors. Suddenly we found ourselves unexpectedly at the forefront of a new form of technology. As an agricultural engineer by training, Jeff was well acquainted with tractor equipment so we decided to design and build the machine ourselves and win the contract. Once we had finished our day jobs at Lambretta, I would ferry wood and steel parts on the roof of my little Morris back to my father's workshop garage at Throwley House School, Strood, in North Kent. Working through the night and on weekends, the first 'McMullan–Smith' fertiliser unit was completed and ready for use in a matter of weeks. We each earned £12 net. Unlikely as it might seem now, this was a lot of money at the time and certainly for us. More importantly, we had gained enormous confidence in our joint abilities to improvise, invent and pull together. A partnership for life had been truly forged.

# Chapter 2

# Axles, Babies and Bills

An exhausting work pattern had developed, as Jeff and I pursued our joint objectives to establish a successful business of our own and, crucially, make some much-needed money. After a full day's work at the Lambretta Croydon factory, we would make the hour-long drive to Throwley House in Strood, where we would labour away on our own projects, often until midnight.

I was newly married and finding it difficult to make ends meet. As a recently qualified doctor, my wife Maureen was working at Westhill Hospital, Dartford, bringing in just £30 a month after tax, compulsory residential costs, etc. A second car for her was out of the question, so we had to find a place to live which was on a bus route, so that she could travel by public transport to the hospital. That 'place' turned out to be a small flat in Bexleyheath, on the Crayford telephone exchange. This seemingly unimportant fact was to play a huge part in our lives, as *Crayford* was to become our business name.

My business partner to be, Jeff, was also having money problems, which were indeed to plague him throughout his life. As the years passed, I could see that this was a common trait among skilled and innovative engineers such as Jeff, whose minds were more often than not elsewhere. Working closely together as we did, I always could tell when the bills for school fees arrived – out of the blue, as far he was concerned – and on those occasions I was under pressure to produce some 'money magic', in the form of an envelope discreetly placed in his overall pocket.

Our first complex engineering project was to produce what was known as a 'live' rear axle for karts. For technical reasons, Lambretta flatly refused to put one into production, so we worked on the development of our own version. The need for a live axle was urgent and necessary: we were changing from high revving twin engines (where it was an advantage for the inside wheel to spin on bends and thus push the engine up the power band) to flat torque motors, where the tyre was required to be in contact with the ground surface at all times.

We came up with the design for this axle, using a firm in Dartford to undertake the production work. Jeff carried out most of the experimental design in the Lambretta Experimental Shop, mostly during his lunch breaks. Once the axle went into production, I was assembling the parts at night in the Throwley House workshop and then despatching the completed units to customers on Saturday mornings from the Post Office in Crayford.

One day in August 1962, on our way to the workshop in Strood for a welding session on our prototype convertible, we had called on my wife, who was heavily pregnant with our first child. Supper in our little flat at Pinnacle Hill, Bexleyheath, over, Maureen remarked in her usual understated, matter-of-fact medical fashion, that if we cared to hang around for a few hours we might just be able to help bring something other than a four-wheeled convertible into the world. Jeff, who had an aversion to anything medical or surgical, was so alarmed and unnerved by the prospect, that he virtually fell headlong down the stairs, tumbling feet first out of the front door. Bruised but invigorated, he went on to finish Crayford's first chassis installation that evening with me.

In the midst of this frantic, almost round-the-clock production activity, I returned from the Croydon factory the next day to learn that my wife had 'changed jobs'. In fact, she had moved from the operating theatre at Westhill Hospital to the Maternity Ward. Maureen, the surgeon, had become a 'working mother' and had given birth to our first baby son, Peter, in the presence, I might add, of most of her hospital colleagues. Later she would recall that almost everyone, bar the hospital security guard, was in the delivery-room audience!

The plan was to build up our sideline business to a commercially viable level before giving up our full-time jobs and putting the Mini into production. I finally left Lambretta in 1963 to team up with Jeff on a full-time basis, working out of the village of Tatsfield, near Westerham. Our modest joint operation was launched using two separate lock-up garages. Unlikely locations and perhaps unlikely beginnings, but persistence and sheer hard work had paid off. By 1964, only a year later, our Crayford Mini sales were booming. That same year we launched the Crayford Cortina Convertible Mk1 at the Racing Car Show in Olympia and to our delight no fewer than 30 were ordered as a taxi hire fleet for Bermuda.

The Ford Corsair Convertible – arguably the best looking of all Crayford conversions – was launched the following year, 1965.

More than 100 were sold, along with 19 cabriolets. Crayford had really taken off. At the peak of our conversion and engine installation business in the late 1970s, we had a staff of 35 on our books and were exporting convertibles world-wide. The new Crayford Cortina Mark 2 convertible was launched in October 1966 at the Earls Court International Motor Show. It was the company's first appearance at this prestigious event and this conversion, together with that of the Mark 3 Cortina, became Crayford's mainstay bestseller and the core of the business for two decades.

However, just as the opportunities were opening up for us

in the 1960s and 1970s, so also did the technical difficulties and potential commercial hazards. These were experiences which, indirectly, gave us a rare and sometimes uncomfortably close-up view of the sorry state of the British motor industry. The famous DeLorean fiasco was a case in point, illustrating a potential hazard we too could face.

The name of John DeLorean, the American entrepreneur, became associated with one of the most disastrous episodes in the history of the UK car trade. But, luckily for us, this is where Jeff's expertise and uncanny insight into the engineering of the business were absolutely invaluable, preventing us from becoming unwittingly involved in one of the most notorious scandals to hit the industry.

A DeLorean representative had indeed approached us with an extraordinary proposal: if we could empty our factory at Westerham and build a prototype model for them, we would be able to write our own cheque, albeit at the British taxpayers' expense as it turned out. They were offering us unlimited funds to get their product up and running, the prototype constructed and operational within a matter of 8 weeks, all in time for the widely anticipated press launch.

Mission impossible, clearly, and Jeff dismissed the whole idea in characteristically robust terms. He wouldn't touch the plan with the proverbial 'barge pole'. How right he was. DeLorean and his associate Colin Chapman ultimately walked away with millions of taxpayers' money, and the project collapsed, amid much anger and political controversy.

At the time it seemed astonishing to us, viewing it from our modest operation in Kent, that the top experts and highly paid civil servants in Whitehall could make such a catastrophic mistake, throwing huge sums of public money into a project which was so obviously a costly non-starter. It had disaster written all over it. And this is not spoken with hindsight, it was staring us in the face at the time.

Another much-publicised howler – the Triumph Stag –

happened around the same time. An absurdly hyped-up piece of promotion appeared in a Sunday newspaper: 'Mercedes look out here comes the Stag! ' This advertisement remained pinned on our office wall for years – by Jeff, as a reminder of how NOT to launch a product. His prediction that the Stag would have major quality problems proved correct. Indeed, some of the models were so defective that their owners were forced to throw away the engines and replace them with other motors. We bought a new Triumph Stag for my wife Maureen to use in her medical practice. It developed an electrical fault and I can still remember Jeffrey holding up a cluster of wires that had been joined together with ordinary PVC electrical tape. Unforgiveable.

We tried to stay all-British with our conversions, but it was an uphill struggle that severely tested our loyalty to home-produced models. BMC and Leyland products, in particular, gave us major headaches – nightmares even. Vehicles such as the Allegro were leaking rainwater before we had even begun to turn them into convertibles. This problem gave rise to a familiar remedying procedure and a crude piece of mechanical surgery at that. When an Allegro arrived at our Westerham factory, one of our engineers would hammer a point-sharpened screwdriver through the floor, thereby enabling the water inside the car to drain away before we began the dismantling and rebuilding operation.

When our first Allegro arrived, we were warned by the police, who used some in their fleet – to avoid jacking the car up on one corner, as this could result in the front windscreen falling out! This warning made us look seriously at what is known as body torsional stiffness. As it turned out, even when we put in place a massive chassis, we found that the car had a tendency to shake like a leaf. In despair, Jeff threatened to fill the vehicle floor with chicken wire and 'Readymix' concrete.

It was just that, though, a threat. However, that reaction was nothing compared with his unprintable response when the first cars in the Allegro batch came down from the Longbridge factory in the West Midlands, sporting square steering wheels.

For us that marked the end of the road. It had been a painful experience and after making 17 we decided to give up on the Allegro as a candidate for conversion – a case of a business going square rather than pear-shaped. Other Leyland 'horrors' emerged, most notably the TR7 Sports. We only built one as a sports estate car model and this was just as well. The original 'build quality' was wretched. In all, it came as no surprise to us later to learn that many TR7 owners in the US had formed an action group to take Leyland to court.

*Converting the TR7 to a prototype sportswagon*

We also went to work with the Princess hatchback. Despite its suggestive tag of royal exclusivity, the Austin Princess was let down by the same problem – poor 'build quality'. Although the basic engineering concept was good and the handling of the car outstanding, parts simply fell off. Not surprisingly, the second-hand values of the vehicles went through the floor. One new 2200 version gave us so much trouble that we were forced to give it to one of our customers in exchange for some steel tubing.

In many ways we paid a heavy price for our close relationship with the deeply troubled British car industry. It was sliding irreversibly downhill, not through lack of engineering skill, which was there in abundance, but through their inability to deliver quality to the customer. In those days, though, 'quality control battles' were often bitterly contested and hard-won issues. This was even the case in our own Westerham factory.

At one point in the mid-1970s I recall watching with dismay as a fitter clearly put a steering wheel on a Mercedes Estate conversion in an impossibly crooked position. When I pointed this out to him the reply I received was negative in the extreme; symptomatic, alas, of what we and no doubt others in the industry had to endure at the time. Yet, thinking back today, I do not think that a 'them' and 'us' accusation could have been levelled at us by our small and compact workforce. There was neither the time nor any desire for such patronising attitudes. In an operation of our kind, working together closely, especially with Jeff as chief engineer, was essential. The only way we could succeed with our sort of intensive 'hands-on' operation was in harmony with our staff. As the business developed, I would work on production on a daily basis, until the coffee break at least, and then move over to the office to tackle the pressing administrative side of the business.

*Jeff Smith in a Motor Show Crayford convertible with a Ford Main Dealer*

*Proud of the original Mini convertible*

# Chapter 3

# Major Worries – Mini Troubles

Work on the Mini had already started during our 'moonlighting' days. All through this time we had been working closely with Ken Wigley, who ran a successful engineering business at Leatherhead, Surrey. From there he undertook the initial roof cut and chassis installation work for us. He was a nice guy to work with and the arrangement went well, though there were some notable hiccups.

The arrangement underpinning our partnership was straightforward. Once a dealer had ordered a car conversion, then we would pass the job over for the initial work to Leatherhead and Crayford–Wigley, as the company became known. We would then collect the completed open-topped vehicle from Leatherhead and drive it to Jeff's small, one-car home garage for the paint work and final completion.

Not everything went according to plan, though. On one occasion, Ken called us to say that the latest car was 'finished' and ready for collection. This was puzzling – we had not been expecting one! Then he told us that he'd found the vehicle, with keys in the ignition, at his front gate and had assumed that the delivery driver had parked it there for him to find and carry out the necessary work. He had done just that and fitted the conversion chassis and cut off the top of the car.

Sleepless nights followed, as we expected an irate owner from Leatherhead to turn up any minute complaining about his decapitated Mini. But, luckily for us, all was well. Eventually, we heard from a dealer who informed us that the car had been sent direct from the factory to Leatherhead and they had forgotten to notify us.

There was another 'Leyland mistake', however, that we never truly unravelled. Two new deluxe Minis were delivered direct from the factory, but without any covering paperwork. They sat in Jeff's front garden for months. Despite countless letters to Leyland, giving all details including chassis numbers, there was no response. It was almost as if the cars didn't exist, which in a sense they didn't, as they were no doubt vehicles which had been built 'on the quiet', products of unauthorised production, which had raised suspicions and questions and now needed to be dumped. As the condition of the vehicles was rapidly deteriorating we decided to register them and began using them. I have no idea where they ended up.

In that same warehouse was another car, memorable, but for all the wrong reasons. We had heard on the grapevine that the last MG Midget was about to come off the production line and Jeff decided that we should buy it and keep the two-seater in store for his daughter, Cath, when she reached her 21st birthday. Later, though, he suddenly decided to sell it, perhaps after noting how the other two Minis had rapidly deteriorated in storage. Polished up and gleaming red with a new battery, it was sold to a MG 'fanatic', delighted to be able to purchase it at the normal retail price. To our dismay, though – and his – the MG turned out to be just about the most unreliable motor put on wheels. So poorly built that he threatened us with legal action. Leyland flatly refused to have anything to do with the matter, so we were left to carry out extensive repairs at our own cost.

The Heinz Hornet deal with the Heinz 57 Food Company in 1965 was an important landmark in the growth of our business.

Looking back now, I can say that it was a project which really established our position in the market. The story of how it all came about is an interesting one. It would seem that one of the Heinz company directors had come up with the idea for the project after having seen our Crayford Mini convertible in the celebrated MGM film *Night Must Fall*, starring Albert Finney and Susan Hampshire. The Heinz 57 Food Company decided to have 57 Wolseley Hornets built as convertibles and give them away in a major promotional competition. A dream order indeed!

*Heinz 57 prize cars helped pay for the factory*

We tried to fix up a meeting in London, but Heinz insisted on sending 3 staff members to our 'factory'. No doubt, they were keen to satisfy themselves that we could actually handle an order of that size. This caused us quite a headache. Our 'factory' at that time was still Jeff's one-car garage at the side of his house in Old Lane and my own newly-built two-car garage down the road in the same village of Tatsfield. Our first meeting took place in the dining room at my home and then we took the delegation out to nearby Biggin Hill for a 'working lunch' in a greasy-spoon caff, housed in a converted private bungalow. Needless to say, the food was dreadful and the 'caff' freezing cold, but they were not put off and we won the order to produce 57 convertibles. They decided, however, to delay the competition for a year, to give us sufficient time to build the vehicles. These Heinz Hornets have since become valuable collectors' items.

Our restricted working premises were causing quite a few problems with deliveries. When the Leyland transporters, fully laden with vehicles, searched for the Tatsfield 'factory' they were somewhat surprised when they finally found us. Inevitably, they caused a total blockage of the narrow village lane outside my house as they unloaded. We were growing fast and things came to a crisis point in the winter of 1965, when there was simply no space left to keep the vehicles. The only possibility was to approach the owner of a heavily wooded and discreet area on the Biggin Hill side of the village for permission to park the cars there, both before and after conversion. The owner actually lived in the woods and was happy to agree to our request. However, a surprise was in store for us. Only when the warming rays of summer arrived did it dawn on us that the impromptu, but very secluded parking lot was home to a nudist colony. It had all the elements of a classic *Carry On* film and ribald comments were rife when word got round the village about the Hornets landing! This was not quite the exposure we had expected ….

As often happens with fast-growing small businesses, we were forced into instant innovation and makeshift yet workable arrangements in order to cope with the Heinz order. It was a totally unexpected business breakthrough, giving us terrific exposure, but at the same time created demands which immediately stretched our flimsy resources to the limit. We had to think fast on our feet.

Buoyed up by the prospect of sudden success, we pressed ahead, employing local craftsmen from the village for different aspects of the work, which was mostly carried out from both our garages. The Heinz order was a great spur and the profits from the project paid for the deposit on the purchase of a former print works, with an attached listed cottage, in Westerham. This was to become our new factory with the name *Crayford Auto Developments Ltd.* being formally registered in 1966.

Generally, though, earning our living was an uphill business, and those early days tested our families as much as they did us. The demands placed on everyone called for immense patience and flexibility. At one point – it was mid-winter in 1966 – Maureen and I had driven over in a new Mini to the Leatherhead garage, where Ken Wigley was installing a chassis for us. The hour-long return journey was unimaginably cold and uncomfortable. By that time it was night and we were driving two open-topped models, without any front- or sidescreens. On arriving back home poor Maureen's face was virtually freeze-dried. Yet this episode epitomised her grit and determination, qualities which made a huge impression on me and were of immeasurable help to me in those early, difficult days. In addition, my resolute 'ice' maiden in that topless motor was heavily pregnant again, expecting our third child, Sarah, the following month.

By this time Maureen had moved into general practice at West Wickham, a few miles north of our home in Tatsfield. Despite all their other working and family commitments, both Maureen and Jeffrey's wife Mary, a pharmacist, worked all the hours they could to help us through the difficult months which followed. As a group we made a tightly-knit working foursome, bringing together a range of valuable skills, most evident when the girls joined us for our monthly financial analysis meetings.

*Mercedes 114 Estate with the Crayford logo by the number plate*

# Chapter 4

# Sunbeds – Overheated Times

In our never-ending search to keep solvent, diversification proved to be our key goal. It was a quest that resulted in some quite unlikely commercial projects. The sunbed adventure, known as *Crayford* Sunstream, was a case in point. In those days the promotional advertising rather quaintly vaunted that sunbeds 'made you brown all over'. We had linked up with a factory producing sunbeds in Germany and arranged for a batch to be brought over. We had taken a stand at the Ideal Homes Exhibition in Olympia. But, not long after we had printed the necessary literature, we discovered that another English firm had copied the idea and we were truly 'nailed'. We could have mounted a challenge to them in the courts, as they were making exact copies. We considered going down this road and taking it to court, but realised that this would have taken three or four years, and quite apart from the sheer waste of time and effort, it could have cost us thousands of pounds in legal fees. Eventually, we decided to throw in the towel and look around for something else. That's when we moved into the stoves trade.

On a trip to Javea, on the Spanish Costa Blanca, we spotted a very cheaply priced woodburning stove. We ordered four, with the intention of using them for what was by then our factory in Tatsfield – Jeff's garage – and also to heat my new two-car workshop/garage. When the stoves arrived, several of our staff wanted to buy them as well and so we purchased a further half dozen. Suddenly, a business opportunity seemed to be opening up. Ex-works, the stoves cost us £13 each plus about £12 for transport to Westerham. We sold them by direct mail at £69 each and after a few years we even persuaded the producers in Albacete to put our name *Crayford* on the lids. This soon grew into a going concern and, as it developed, we exercised re-exporting rights for other countries.

However, technically, there were certain problems with the stoves which needed to be resolved. Made from thin sheet metal, instead of cast iron, they wasted a remarkable amount of heat by throwing it both downwards as well as outwards.

Customers were warned in the instructions supplied with the stoves that they should layer two inches of sand into the bottom of the unit to prevent the heat burning a hole in the floor beneath. Not everyone took notice of this advice and several boat owners, using them on board their vessels, found they had created unwanted underwater portholes! One client ran a nursery at the end of Chestnut Avenue, where Jeff lived. A panic call came through: one of the stoves seemed to be falling apart. Jeff dashed over to deal with the emergency, only to find that the heat generated had reached such a high temperature that the legs were almost falling off. Moreover, the metal walls were so thin, flames were visible from outside the greenhouse. More than 20 years on, (December 2004), when I called in on that same garden centre, the owner told me that he still had vivid memories of that celebrated over-heated occasion.

Normally the stoves were delivered by a Spanish transport specialist. From time to time, however, we sent over our own VW van to make a collection ourselves. On one occasion, as a short holiday break, Maureen and Mary (Jeff's wife) offered to do the long transportation run. Later it became clear that these intrepid ladies had endured a trying and tiresome journey. A quick check on the high fuel consumption later revealed that for most of the way to Spain and back the van had been driven in second gear – a pardonable error, perhaps, because the vehicle had a relatively silent automatic transmission unit, located under the floor at the rear end of the vehicle, and thus well out of earshot.

Although these sideline operations of ours came and went over the years, they were essentially driven by a basic commercial philosophy: to promote a product with wide market potential. The overseas openings were the key and always had to be taken on board. The guiding rule of thumb was: will it sell in Capetown and Chicago, or Montreal, Mombasa and Melbourne? Commercial attachés were, of course, based in British Embassies worldwide and it was their job to assist people such as ourselves to export – aid provided at no cost. Then there was the British Society of Motor Manufacturers (the SMMT), who ran low-cost trade missions to help introduce British products on a global scale.

I went on one of the SMMT missions to Johannesburg in the late 70s and was introduced to the director of a South African specialist auto-body builder at an embassy reception. (The same contact also introduced me to the joys of a whole range of excellent South African wines). That initial three-hour long embassy conversation, devoted wholly to the subject of cars, led to a visit from the firm's engineer to study our method of building the Mercedes Estate as a conversion model – at that time the only one of its kind in the world. We then agreed to grant the company the production licence rights for South Africa, with our company shipping out to them the glass, roof panels, jigs and various other parts when required. Encouraged by this development, we turned our attention to the Australian and US markets, where Mercedes were selling in volume. As a result, we became close friends with Harpers of Detroit, who took on the manufacturing licence in a similar way.

This kind of licence arrangement was profitable and easy to set up. But it did call for a key requirement: qualification as an Original Equipment (OE) operation. To the layman, this might pose an obvious question – why would an overseas firm not simply copy an original design? The answer is that such a move could be risky and trigger legal action, as well as the manufacturer's refusal to grant the manufacturer's warranty approval, as originators of the conversion. In any event, in a legitimate arrangement, involving something in the order of a £50 licence fee per car, an overseas firm automatically received all the necessary design drawings, tools, technical co-operation and know-how backup.

The Mini convertible was our first overseas licensing operation, where we were despatching parts to Australia, via a Sydney-based importer. It was not an auspicious start, as nothing further was heard after despatch – not until some years later that is. A call came through from Australia and we learnt that the Mini chassis units were still in the docks there and although payment had been made for the kit parts, the importer had disappeared without trace. After lengthy negotiations we arranged for the kits to be returned to Britain and later made good use of them in further conversions.

# Chapter 5

# Bullet-proof Mercedes

Amidst this roller coaster ride to the commercial success we ultimately achieved, there were also hard times, and nothing reminds me more of the early days struggle than a certain roadside phone box just outside Tunbridge Wells in Kent.

When business was bad and there were no cars waiting for conversion, Jeff and I would attend a second-hand car auction, held every Tuesday in this old spa town. We were looking to buy something cheap for refurbishment, usually a Morris 1000 or similar model. As soon as a bid was successful I would have to make a call from this particular phone kiosk, to place a 'for sale' ad for the car we had not yet driven back to our own garage base. The closing time for ads imposed a tight deadline, but they were tight times and this called for urgent, drastic measures to keep our business afloat. Once home, we then had two days to fix whatever was wrong with the vehicle and prepare it for re-sale. The basic rule was simple – buy cheap, no matter what.

The car auction experience was important for more than one reason: we had to think fast on our feet. First we did a quick pre-estimate of the prices of vehicles at the auction and then followed the proceedings to see what 'clangers' we had dropped. It was a sharp learning curve, this, in the art of calculating prices and gauging prospective market potential in what was always a difficult and highly competitive business.

It was during this phase of rapid turnover dealings that we stumbled across a celebrated vehicle full of trouble – a local mobile fish ’n chips van. It was going cheap, but there was a persistent fish smell and wavy blue lines on its side panels. We tried to remove the unmistakable chip-shop odour by opening all its doors and exposing it to the elements. Parked discreetly at the bottom of my garden, it underwent this air-freshening treatment for a whole three months. To no avail, though. And there were further problems. To our dismay, John Panther, our painter and friend, was unable to completely hide the blue line logo, despite every effort and successive coats of paint. Finally, we sold it to a Welsh undergraduate in Camberwell, who had been suffering from a heavy head cold at the time!

Some of our car-selling operations in the late 1970s took us quite unexpectedly into an almost surreal cloak-and-dagger world. None more so than the sale of the bullet-proof Mercedes, which we had originally built ‘on spec’. We had no specific customer in mind. But because it was bullet-proofed and not everyone’s cup of tea, it was for sale at an accessible price – possibly also because of its colour – it was yellow. We ran ads for months, but totally failed to find a buyer. It was valued at £75,000 and finally, in desperation, we put the car into auction with the instruction that we would accept a bottom price of £40,000. This was a knock-down price, which was going to hit us badly. When the bids halted at £30,000, the auctioneer announced he would check to see if we would accept. When later we told him we would indeed agree to that bid, we were told there had been no offers in the auction room. It turned out they were simply bids ‘taken off the wall’ – a not uncommon practice, it seems, to stimulate interest amongst the bidders present.

The Mercedes fiasco had caused our finances serious

damage and we were now in a financial hole of grave proportions. And then, remarkably, seemingly out of the blue, we received a call from a cash customer in the form of a leading London merchant bank looking for – you name it – a bullet-proof Mercedes! The managing director himself instructed me to come to his City office the next day to collect a cheque from his secretary, which I did. It was a bank draft for £75,000 – an instant sale although, oddly, no-one representing the purchaser had even viewed, let alone examined, the vehicle. Maybe our reputation had travelled further than we realised. The instructions were as simple as they were mystifying: 'place the Mercedes in a sealed container and despatch it to Mexico City.'

Marketing rules suggest that, in any line of business, the first sale is the toughest. So, I set about trying to turn one deal into two. Maureen and I visited close friends, the Cramptons, who had settled in Mexico City to do medical research. Deep down I harboured the hope that whilst there I might identify the new owner of our bullet-proof Mercedes – maybe even sell another one. However, I failed to trace the car, despite handing out ten dollar bills to local taxi drivers, in the vain hope of picking up some clues. Even if the vehicle had been resprayed, the wheels would have been immediately identifiable to us: we had fitted it with special wheels and tyres which could withstand high-velocity fire and enable the car to get away, travelling at 60 mph.

Calls to the merchant bank in London failed to elicit any further information, other than that the car was 'fine' and could we supply the original wing mirrors. We had removed these and sealed up the holes as part of the bullet-proofing measures. Any 'bolt-through' component represented a weakness in the vehicle skin and we were aware from our research that a skilled marksman with a rifle on a tripod could put three or four 7.62mm bullets through the same weak spot.

From Mexico City, on a long-distance call, I ordered a

pair of mirrors for despatch to a box number in the Mexican capital.

It was only to be expected that the 'bullet-proofing' years would bring both drama and technical problems. We were dealing with Mercedes models, though, and both of us greatly admired the engineering work which went into the production of these cars. After years of building estate and convertibles, we were very familiar with the model and its capabilities.

This was another world: the vehicle specifications were linked to the various levels of threat – ranging from those posed by a small handgun or revolver to the high velocity rifle, capable of putting six shots in six seconds into a victim's head from a distance of up to 500 yards. The customers always insisted upon the highest level of secrecy both with regard to their own identity and the vehicle specifications. New clients always demanded to know all our conversion 'secrets' before placing an order. In one instance, a well known bank in a north Spanish city, with strong British connections, sent over a delegation to check us out and supervise rigorous firing tests. The visiting group also included a marksman travelling with his own rifle. Quite how he managed to get through the security checks at Heathrow remains a mystery.

This order required us to build a full bullet-proof Mercedes door for test firing. The bank's security advisors also demanded a test on the windscreen, which we set up – the glass alone costing £5,000 – at a shooting range in North London. We stood by, watching as their weapons expert destroyed it.

When billed afterwards for £10,000 the bank responded immediately with a cheque by return post. These Spanish clients also sought assurances and proof on vehicle handling and performance. This was an area of technical difficulty in view of the huge weight increase, resulting from the conversion work. The model was then test driven by their own specialist driver. For a full hour he put one of our vehicles (the spectacular yellow model later bound for Mexico) through its screeching paces along the narrow, winding lanes of north Kent. Our staff promptly gave him the nickname of 'Fangio', after the great Argentine racing driver.

As far as our American clients were concerned, the weight factor and performance issues were less of a problem. They had been 'stretching' cars for years and had overcome the braking power hurdles. Yet, to us, this tricky technical area constituted a staggering problem, more of a nightmare in fact.

Thankfully, the Mercedes staff in London were very helpful and, if ultimately unable to assist, they would always contact 'Experimental' at their German HQ for advice. Upgrading the brakes to cope with the huge increase in vehicle weight was quite the most formidable challenge. With this outside guidance, however, we managed it.

We were fitting what was known as an 'attack location' device inside these cars. It was a form of radar, which in the event of an assault gave instant information about the direction from which fire was coming, enabling the driver to take evasive action. But other worrying factors still had to be taken into account, because even our 2 inch armoured front windscreens would let through a $4^{th}$ or $5^{th}$ bullet, if shots were aimed within a 5 inch space of each other.

One unpleasant side issue arising from the complexities and challenges of 'armouring' was known, somewhat graphically, as the 'colander syndrome'. In the case of a conventional vehicle with normal steel panelling, a single bullet might simply travel straight through and, with luck, disappear harmlessly out the other side. But quite another set of problems arise with an armoured vehicle in the case of a so-called 'hose-down' of heavy automatic fire. In such circumstances, just one single penetration can have a devastating effect once inside the passenger compartment. The bullet, unable to exit, ricochets around the interior, not unlike an irate wasp, with deadly consequences.

These were some of the challenging practical issues confronting the specialist arm of our business, *Crayford*

*Armouring Ltd.* as it was known. Indeed, we soon became well known among the other companies involved in this highly specialised field of conversion, sharing problems with them and swapping tales and experiences.

One such company, based in Wales and renowned for its excellent work told us of an especially frightening experience, which was to have a profound effect on our general approach to this part of our business. They had supplied a fleet of bullet-proof Land Rovers to an East African state, with their sales manager accompanying the vehicle delivery. On arrival at their airport, to his horror, the customer told him they would need to test fire one of the Land Rovers before making the payment. Furthermore, on the customer's insistence, he would have to sit inside the vehicle whilst it was sprayed with automatic gunfire. Shades of Evelyn Waugh's *Scoop*! It was precisely this kind of experience which ultimately persuaded us to drop out of the bullet-proofing business....

Another worrying factor which led to this decision was the risk of 'retaliation' by associates of African and Middle Eastern clients, should things go disastrously wrong and a leader be killed in one of our vehicles. Also, our own workmanship was perceived to be in question.

International news took on an unexpectedly new dimension in our lives. On one occasion we had spent weeks preparing a bullet-proofed Mercedes for shipment to the Yemen and the delivery went to plan. One weekend sometime later, while reading the papers outside our chalet at Sheerness, Maureen asked me where the latest Mercedes had been shipped to and for whom. For the President,' I replied. Her answer gave me quite a shock. 'Well, he won't be needing that any more. He's just been assassinated!'

A few worrying days followed as I pondered on whether or not our Yemeni contacts would be sending a visitor to discuss the quality – or perceived lack of it – of our armouring work. As it turned out, the presidential victim was the head of state of a different part of Yemen. But, in a volatile world of political intrigue and violence, the consequences of working on such contracts were becoming a source of growing concern.

In truth, the bullet-proofing business was also becoming unattractive for a number of other reasons. Sourcing the type of glass we needed was fraught with problems. We had always used armoured material (costing £5,000 a time) manufactured by one of the UK's leading suppliers. Similar top quality screens of German origin were even more expensive and uneconomical. Although the British versions possessed good test firing capabilities, their shape was always unsatisfactory, meaning that we were forced to set the front windscreen in place on the Mercedes and then reshape the new car windscreen aperture to conform to the dimensions of the poorly constructed screen.

Armouring was also taking yet another turn, in a way which made it an even less attractive proposition. The profit and growth potential of the business was attracting the 'wide boys' on the fringes of the car business. Until now we had been used to dealing with the main Mercedes, Leyland and Ford dealerships Europewide. Then, suddenly, this was a world peopled by some distinctly unsavoury gentlemen.

On one occasion we were approached with the promise of an order, but on one condition that an advance payment of £10,000 be made to a contact, an Arab go-between as it turned out. Desperate, I sought immediate advice and guidance. How would the Inland Revenue react to the appearance of such a sum in our books, simultaneous with a substantial motor sale to which it was so clearly linked ? I was advised that the inspector would automatically connect the two, yet still probably accept the dual deal without question, for the simple reason that it was an acceptably common occurrance. And that's precisely how it worked out. I handed over a briefcase full of money at a meeting in a Kensington hotel. But it was a deal which left us feeling distinctly uneasy and less than comfortable.

*A Mercedes 450 Condor*

*BMC 1100/1300 hatchback conversion: one of the first in Britain. It enjoyed a production run of 5 a week for many years*

# Chapter 6

# The Taxman Cometh

Jeff and I were always sensitive and wary of anything that might be deemed illegal or could in any way cause problems. We were fortunate to have sound and authoritative advice from our accountants, the late Ian MacDonald and then his partner, Jim Thompson, still a valued friend. Both played a significant role in the development of Crayford, by providing their sound advice and financial expertise.

It was as a result of an accidental, but fortuitous, meeting at St. Alfeges Hospital, South East London, where Maureen was first employed as a junior surgeon in 1961, that I teamed up with Ian MacDonald. I often had to wait there for hours for my wife to finish work and one day I was trying to open a window in the unbearably overheated doctor's lounge area. The overworked heating facility was the most impressive aspect of the system, although it did raise questions as to how the NHS could justify such wasteful extravagance. Despite my efforts, the window would not yield and a large, friendly Scot, Ian MacDonald, came over to give me a hand. As we did so, we looked down at the car park below and discovered that we both were driving Morris Minor 1000 models. Further, it transpired that Ian, a newly qualified accountant, was also waiting for his wife to finish. She was the anaesthetist working with Maureen in the same operating theatre. We talked about cars and careers and I told him I was thinking of starting my own engineering business. 'What a coincidence', he replied. 'I am about to start my own accountancy practice'. Almost jokingly, it was agreed that if my company came into being, I would be his first client. And that is the way events turned out.

Way back then it would never have occurred to us that, years later, millions of pounds were to pass through our hands nor that we would be meeting for monthly working lunches in expensive restaurants to discuss our accounts. Nor that in adjacent car parks would be two fine Mercedes, symbols of the success we had both achieved. The struggling years and the days of driving Mini Minors were by then a distant memory only.

Ian was a true Scottish accountant, with an acute sense of what was or wasn't allowable. In that sense he was tougher on us than the Inland Revenue or the VAT inspector themselves. If at any point I suggested resorting to a somewhat 'grey area' accounting procedure as a means of reducing our tax bill, he would look at me with a knowing smile. 'David', he'd say, 'don't even think about it. They spend their whole lives learning to spot naughties.' Sometimes, when I came up with what I considered to be a clever and, to me, seemingly 'non-naughty' tax offsetting ploy, he would bury his head in his hands and simply laugh.

Early on I learnt from this canny Scot that, in this context at least, a good pro always beats a good amateur and that the Inland Revenue inspectors enjoyed two principal advantages: they were trained for the job and, perhaps less obviously, time was always on their side. This aspect was important, as later events confirmed. We had been warned that if an item in the books looked at all 'fishy' they might appear to ignore it for a year or two. Such difficulties were all the more evident in the second-hand car business where VAT and part-exchange figures varied with every deal.

We established a good relationship with all civil servants, including the VAT inspector. He was a charming Scot, known to us all as 'John the VAT' . We may have crossed swords with him on a few occasions over some silly error or other, but we always ended up next door in the Royal Standard pub, where earlier misunderstandings were sorted out amicably over a whisky or two. Indeed, it became obvious to me that, if dealt with properly, the Revenue, VAT and Customs inspectors could actually help us with the accurate monitoring of the running of our business. So much so that when, in later years, national budget cuts made their visits less frequent, I would phone the Redhill, Surrey, VAT office to find out why we hadn't received the usual call from an inspector. We were perhaps unique in this, inviting visits from the VAT man. However, it became clear to us that short term errors hurt much less to correct than those which had unwittingly accrued over a longer period.

For the unwary, unexpected VAT traps could suddenly loom into view. For years I had been in the habit of offering a petrol gift, filling up the fuel tank as a 'thank-you to the customer' – a gesture to Mercedes owners who had approached us direct for a conversion job. During a routine check of the petrol accounts, VATman John had spotted fuel marked 'F.O.C.' (free of charge) on the works charge sheet. 'Very generous of you to give free petrol,' he remarked. 'But what about the VAT?'

We had not realised that by offering free fuel we were in fact giving away HM tax – without any authority to do so. The error was ultimately rectified, based on a reasonable estimate of a few hundred pounds and accepted as a genuine error, but not to be repeated. During a subsequent lunch together at the Royal Standard, the topic of free petrol came up. The eagle-eyed Scotsman peered at me over his whisky and said: 'Make sure you're not giving away any more VAT, won't you?'. It was a timely reminder and rang bells for me, as intended. He had noticed in our books that, as part of a promotion gesture, we'd sent out free woodburning stoves to various outlets. It was a calculated opportunity for me to 'tidy up' the figures, as indeed I did.

This sort of co-operation and understanding was essential at all levels of the business. Mistakes were bound to happen and Jeff would get hot under the collar when something went wrong on the accounting and book-keeping side. And this is where the contrast between the two different worlds we worked in were most marked and what he instinctively sensed and resented. On the practical, mechanical side a problem, however disastrous it seemed at first sight, could be quickly sorted out with a couple of weekends of hard work. But the accounts side of the business was rather more complex, drawn out and yes, ultimately taxing.

# Chapter 7

# Choppy Waters

In the early seventies we started the supply of the Argocat, a highly versatile all-terrain amphibian vehicle with a wide range of uses. The opportunity had come as a result of our Spanish agent introducing us earlier to a Canadian six-wheel amphibious machine of dubious quality, called the Amphicat. One of its problems was that if damp got into the ignition system the engine would start and if the automatic transmission had been left in 'engage' drive, the Amphicat headed off with its six-wheel drive making it almost unstoppable. In very wet weather we would sometimes hear a shriek of laughter from a lady member of staff, who happened to be looking out of the window when an Amphicat suddenly burst into life and created driverless havoc in the car park. I heard that in Canada once one had started up on its own, climbed over everything in sight, then headed across a main road and smashed its way through the huge plate glass window of the car showroom opposite. I had to find an alternative, for there appeared to be a great deal of interest in this type of amphibious vehicle, never seen before in Britain. Eventually I found the Argo – also made in Canada. It too was amphibious and we renamed it the Argocat. After making various alterations it became a huge success for many years.

The Snowgoose was another water craft that became part of the business – a case where we landed up in choppy waters. We had built this boat, which was a catamaran, assuming that we had the right, as a company making an amphibious vehicle (the Argocat), to operate it as a floating 'tender' to supervise the testing of our vehicles. But boats and planes on company accounts attract attention and the Snowgoose was no exception.

After a few years of deliberation, the VAT-Revenue monitors concluded that we had used the catamaran for personal recreation. The issue had become a source of worry, as the authorities were posing questions during an enquiry which lasted for some months. A diversion of some kind was called for. So I designed (for the benefit of HM Customs) a small illustrated leaflet, showing the Snowgoose in use for support work for the Argocat amphibious vehicles.The preparation of the leaflet involved a visit to the Conyer Marina near Teynham, Kent with a camera to photograph the Argocat body being crane-lifted onto our boat.

Yet the all-seeing eyes of those who have 'been there, done that' are seemingly everywhere and never more so than in this area of activity. Amazingly, as this delicate photo-shoot/promotional manoeuvre was taking place, a complete stranger, sipping a cocktail on the cockpit of a nearby boat, shouted across to me: 'The Revenue will never swallow it!' And he was right. The carefully assembled printed leaflet didn't make the slightest difference. Some weeks and not a few sleepless nights later, it was showdown time regarding the disputed vessel. A party of three inspectors arrived at our office in Westerham to discuss the vexed issue….

One of them was especially pedantic and insistent, pressing home the point about our personal recreational use of the catamaran. I explained that we probably sailed no more than eight times during the season. Then I was questioned more closely about how much it would cost to hire the vessel for a weekend. An arbitrary figure was quoted, accepted and our accountant concurred. Then the VAT inquisitor concluded: 'In that case, you have had £1600 worth of boat use and you must pay the VAT and personal tax on that use.' The much-feared meeting was over within 15 minutes, as were the weeks of anguish. We all stood up and moved into the very convenient Royal Standard pub next door to test the whisky or in my case whiskey. An alarming form of scrutiny, but thankfully the only serious one of its kind we were to ever encounter. As such, it was a salutary episode, which frankly taught us not to be too clever in future. All part of the so-called learning curve of practical experience in an area of business where financial and regulatory traps were forever opening up and taking us by surprise.

It was the late Colin Chapman, owner of Lotus and a director of the DeLorean operation, who summed up the prevailing circumstances of the time. 'It was', he said, ' like trying to keep a bucket filled with water while governmental and other forces persistently drilled holes in it', That is indeed just how it seemed at times.

Increased government regulation enforcing various safety measures and strict conditions on the manufacturers of vehicles proved to be a constant nightmare. Fortunately, the British authorities had refused to accept the then new European standards requiring that all passenger cars should be crash tested before they could be registered. Like most other small manufacturers, we at *Crayford* could not possibly afford such an extra burden on our costs. So a typically British compromise was reached.

In our case, it was agreed that, as volume-limited manufacturers, we could be absolved from the requirements of crash testing on one important condition: that Ford and Mercedes agreed to our using their already homologated type approval numbers on certain components. This Ford and Mercedes agreed to do. The homologation conditions were measures designed to ensure the vehicles met certain safety standard requirements. There was another British-negotiated loophole: that manufacturers such as ourselves could convert cars after the point of sale. This was an equally crucial point.

These measures effectively prevented a disaster in our field and the almost inevitable closure of most of the volume manufacturers such as *Crayford*. But, happily, the 'loophole' arrangement did in fact have the reverse effect, stimulating these companies to expand and develop their products. The UK form of opt-out was not available in most other European countries. German regulations, for example, made it an offence for a car to be used on public roads in any form other than as built, or with the officially approved manufacturer's option package. Since then most European countries have followed that policy. The British solution – whereby small manufacturers and private individuals have the right to put on the road whatever they liked, provided the vehicle met basic construction and legal requirements – was a rare case of government wisdom. We were sympathetic to the new safety regulation requirements, but they imposed huge burdens on small manufacturers. So the official British approach was widely appreciated as a measure that combined practical sense and technical logic.

The principal focus of worry in the 'convertible world' was the adoption of the 'roll-over' test, as developed in the 1970s in California. In this punishing hurdle, the vehicle was turned upside down as it left the ramp and then dropped in such a manner that all the weight bore down on one of the front windscreen pillars – the upper A post, in engineering-speak. There was a further demand – a roll-over bar behind the passenger's head and the added requirement that the upper seat belt anchorage had to be at shoulder level. These new regulations were almost universally adopted throughout the 1980s. The safety of cars during an accident had always been a matter of concern, but a new factor had entered the equation:

speed. Family cars had normally been driven at around forty mph until after the second world war. Then suddenly 80 mph was very possible and the death toll had started to rise.

It was in the seventies that it looked as if the incoming regulations being discussed by the British government would put a stop to convertible manufacture world-wide. So it was not surprising that, in view of this very real threat to our convertible business, we were continually on the lookout for other outlets for our production expertise and innovation. This had been the main driver for our move into bullet-proofing and, more particularly, estate car manufacture. And yet, looking back on that difficult period some 30 years or so later, it now seems to me that the various government agencies put us through a good deal of unnecessary business angst. The final outcome was to leave the convertible field almost as it was. But not before we had travelled a long and agonising path in anticipation of stringent new legal requirements.

It should be said that the measures which were introduced to meet some of the anticipated demands were highly inventive. Mercedes, for instance, went a good way towards conforming with the roll bar requirement, by introducing a highly sophisticated bar, which flipped up automatically in the event of an accident. At Crayford, we developed our own version of the roll bar, by incorporating it as part of the roof mechanism. We had no illusions, however, about its effectiveness, and it would never have passed the violent 'inverted drop' test. But our experience, combined with the testimony of many convertible users, strongly suggested that in certain instances, our models offered far more safety features than most of the standard factory models and also gave an acceptably good level of protection in the event of front or rear impact.

There was strong evidence to back this up. I can think of one surprising instance, in particular, when on one occasion we were called by Dees, a main Ford dealer in South Croydon, urging us to come over and look at one of our Crayford Corsair convertibles which had sustained massive frontal damage after hitting a lamp post at speed. The chassis we had installed at floor level had remained absolutely intact; more than that, I seem to recall that, despite the devastating effects of the impact, we were still able to open the doors. Photographic evidence of this survives in archives.

In the face of the demands imposed by the safety regulations affecting our industry, we went ahead with a major conversion project. This was the world's first and only Mercedes Sport SL Station Wagon, which was exhibited at the 1980 National Exhibition Centre Motor Show in Birmingham. During its construction, we spent many hours worrying about a key technical problem – how to return the original torsional 'stiffness' to the vehicle. We knew from experience that Mercedes vehicles give a good firm ride and were the sort of cars which were frequently driven at speed along rough roads, in a variety of testing locations around the world. Our solution to this challenge was to insert a massive roll bar, about halfway back inside the frame, a measure which meant there was very restricted seating for anyone bold enough to be a rear-seat passenger. The incorporation of this roll bar, however, probably saved quite a few lives.

This highly specialised 3-door Mercedes Sport SL Station Wagon was known as the Condor. It was bought by a charming Egyptian doctor. We heard no more until some time later when the owner – an unquestionably satisfied client – surprised us with a request for a total rebuild of the car. It seemed that, miraculously, he had managed to drive the vehicle up a tree in Majorca and supplied a photograph to prove it! The car – and its passengers – had survived more or less intact. But retrieval of the vehicle itself had required drastic surgery, in fact a Spanish solution of an unusual kind: the tree had to be cut down. Back in Westerham we also had our work cut out.

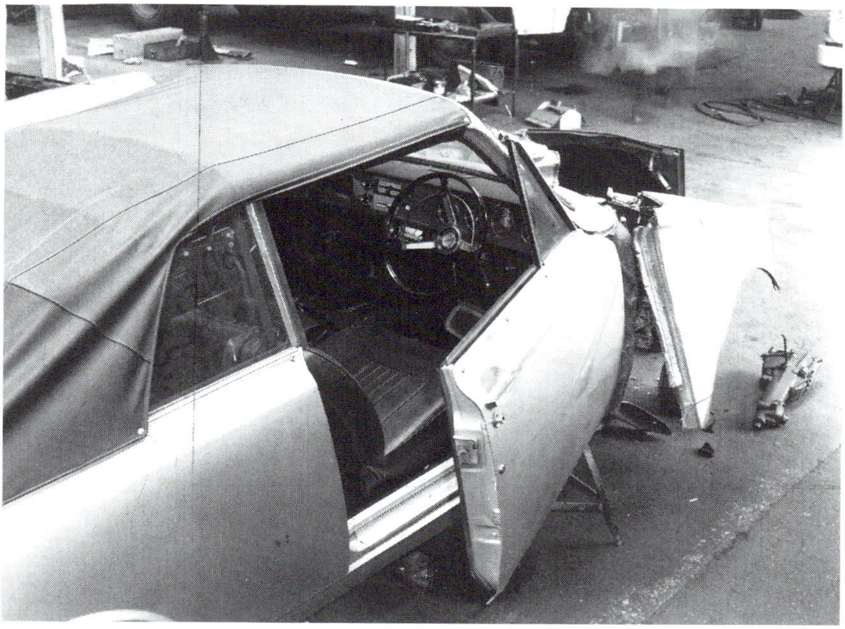

*Dee's Corsair after head-on crash. The sill is intact and the door still opens.*

My son, Sean, then just finishing his engineering apprenticeship, took on the daunting task of returning the Mercedes to its original pre-crash state. Displaying real engineering talent, he did an outstanding job in restoring it to its gleaming, pristine condition – with the skilled help, that is, of our paint-shop craftsman, John Panther. Eventually, the Condor was bought back and remained with *Crayford* for some years, ultimately to become the property of the two motor industry executives, the late David Butlion and David Connold who, on my retirement from the business in 1987, formed a partnership and took over the company, along with its name and worldwide sales franchise. (I was to retain the factory freehold at Westerham, leasing it back to the new owners and finally selling the premises to a local developer for housing in 1990).

*David McMullan inspects a completed MK.4 Cortina outside the fatory at Westerham. Note the rear quarter-light moves down as part of the hood.*

The Ford Cortina convertible continued to feature throughout the history of *Crayford*, (the last Crayford Cortina was made for the national Motor Show in 1980 and based on the all-new 1980 Mk 5 model). The first of our high performance Cortina variants was fitted with a V6 engine, special clutch and suspension. The Press called this animal of a motor 'savage' and so it was. The flexibility and torque of this type of conversion was quite phenomenal, as was its legendary capacity for ripping out gearboxes.

On one memorable occasion, I raced one of the Cortina V6 models along the famous Jabekke Highway, travelling from Brussels to the cross-channel ferry at Ostend at well over 100 mph for most of the journey. Its response to this challenge was indeed savage – the transmission finally exploded within 100 yards of the ferry terminal. Our foreman, travelling in another Crayford, had reached the dock just before me, so as the vessel began to move out of the dock, I swifly locked up the expired Cortina, sprinted across the grass, leapt over the outer rail of the vessel and stepped on board, with no ticket. The abandoned V6 was later picked up by our agent in Belgium.

The V6 attracted great interest in the trade, and not all of it above board – for industrial espionage was not unknown, even then. One morning I peered out of my bedroom window at Ship Hill, Tatsfield, to find the latest V6 I had parked in the driveway the previous night had gone. A call came through from the police a few hours later. The vehicle had been found not far away, in Pilgrim's Way, Westerham. I knew just who had taken it on a pilgrimage – and why. Our engine mounts on the model were acknowledged to be an unrivalled example of top class design and engineering. It was clear that the taking of photographs of the components had been the point and purpose of the take-away exercise. Afterwards, I somehow managed to resist the temptation to call a certain number in Essex, to 'thank' the rival competitor behind the theft for so neatly folding up my travelling rug in such a considerate manner and request a copy of the prints for my own use.

But this was not a world in which gentlemanly irony played much of a role. We were often subject to the overt activities of the so-called 'pretend' customers – usually turning up in pairs to examine the Argocat. Their approach took on a familiar and almost transparent pattern. One of the customers would engage us in conversation whilst a photoman, as we called such interlopers, took shots of everything, but more particularly the engine and transmission layout.

*Promoting the Mercedes 280CE St Tropez Convertible*

# Chapter 8

# Sharpies in Pointed Shoes

We were prepared for espionage and had a decoy system in place, which was worthy of any piece of World War II 'distract-the-enemy' stratagem. On such visits, Jeff would declare to me quite volubly that the new prototype should not be available for photographs. This message was conveyed loudly enough for the visitors to overhear. They then took the bait and somehow conspired to get their pictures. The catch was that the 'new prototype' was nothing of the sort, just an old fibreglass Argo, which we had fitted with a quite useless hydraulic transmission and inadequate diesel engine.

So we soon instinctively knew just when we were being spied upon – it had become a second sense, developed and honed through a hands-on experience of intense rivalry in a fiercely competitive business. One common factor soon surfaced in these close indelicate encounters of the espionage kind: the nearer to London our inquiring 'visitors' were based, the more likely they were to be crooks of one form or another. But there were also very genuine enquiries. In one instance, a couple arrived claiming, oddly enough, that they were from a village garage outside Inverness in Scotland. On another occasion, no less than a team of four inquisitors from Catford,

South London, swooped down on us in a Range Rover. Their obvious problems with the norms of English syntax gave them away almost immediately, as did their pointed shoes. Rough-edged 'sharpies' in wide-boy footwear, for sure, and there were plenty of their ilk snooping around to challenge the unwary and the gullible. Happily, we were neither and came to enjoy these interludes which had become quite entertaining.

One investigation took us by complete surprise, because it came from such an unexpected source. It focussed on our Mercedes Estate conversion method. We had converted a new model of the vehicle for an Arab customer, who collected the car personally for onward shipment to the Middle East via the London Docks. Or so we thought. Several months later we received a bill from a hotel close to the Mercedes factory at Sindelfingen, near Stuttgart. This completely baffled us. We had not visited there for some time and, in any event, never used that particular hotel. We made enquiries and were given the name of the customer who had forgotten to pay his bill. He had accidently left behind one of our business catalogues and it was on the basis of this clue that the hotel had sent the outstanding bill to us. It turned out to be our Arab client, who had by previous arrangement clearly driven the new car straight to the Mercedes Experimental department in Germany.

Evidently, the car had been dismantled for 'quality control' purposes. This was because by then the German company had allowed us limited 'Mercedes warranty' after conversions. This move had been in truth a 'stealth' check to assess our production quality. The information was received in good spirit. A year or so later, one of the senior Mercedes engineers, a charming elderly executive who had become a good friend, called at our stand at a subsequent motor show and we shared a quiet laugh about the whole episode.

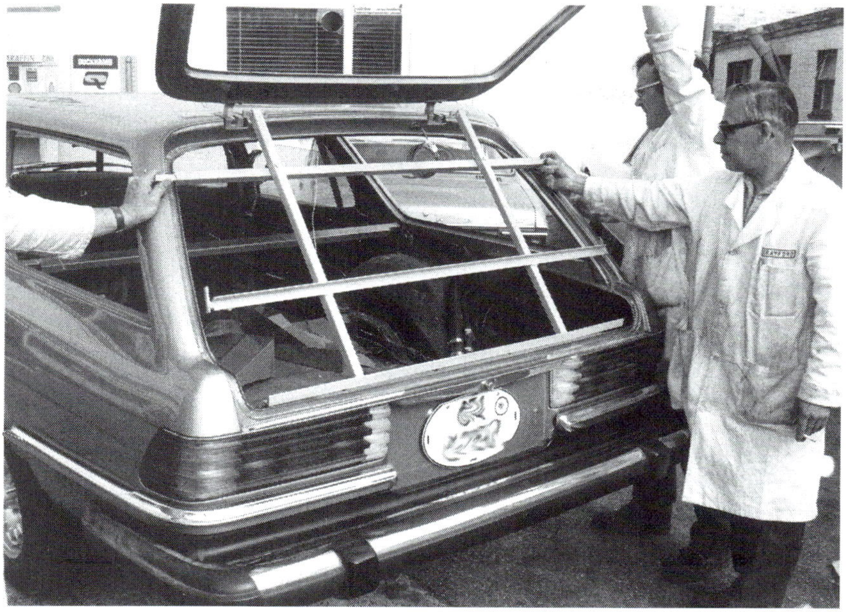

*Working on Sophia Loren's Mercedes S Class Estate*

It had taken us something like ten years to establish our reputation with Mercedes and gain their hard-won confidence. So we accepted, in a good natured way, that they had a vested interest in keeping an eye on us. Only years later was I to discover that one of the senior engineers had used a Crayford Mercedes 280 convertible as his personal car. This was in itself a gratifying endorsement of their confidence in our ability to produce the high quality work which was in keeping with the great Mercedes name.

This reflected the good relationship we enjoyed with the company. The policy was that anything we did to the car with the three pointed star on its bonnet had to be as near to perfection as possible. Our insistence on absolute thoroughness was appreciated by their staff and for this reason we were, at that time, the only engineers in the world allowed to build the Mercedes estates with the highly prized factory warranty still mainly intact.

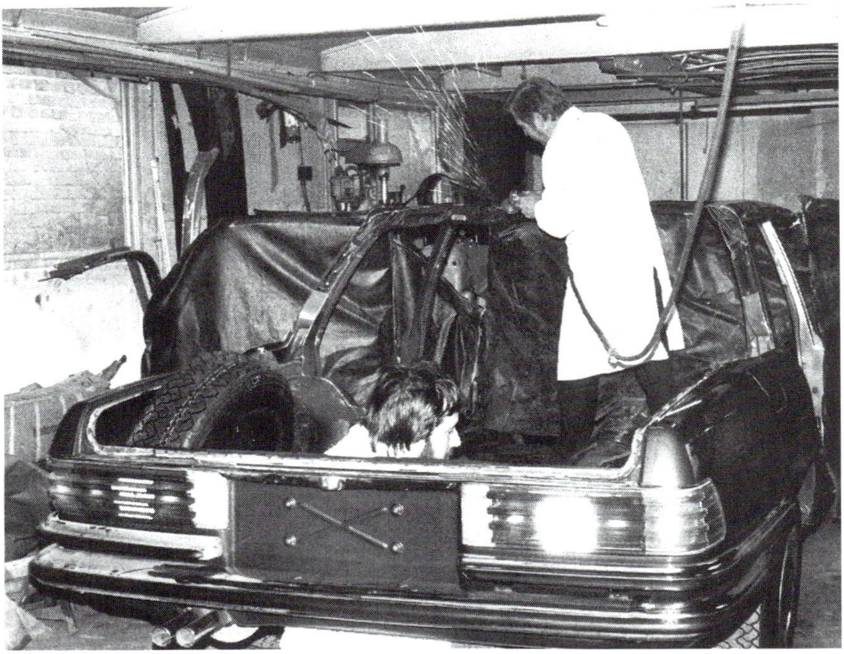

*Work on the Mercedes 450SE Laundette progresses*

Jeff's mantra: 'Near enough is not good enough' earned us a lot of money. The convertibles we built with electro-hydraulic tops were constructed to a standard that was unmatched in Britain. It is true that, at the time, Rolls Royce were building an impressive convertible but, in our estimation, they were using inferior hooding material. We had always sourced our material for the car hoods from Happich of Wuppertal, the German company which had been making this material since before the war.

Like so many German factories, the Happich factory building had been reduced to an empty shell by the onslaught of the RAF Lancaster bombers. After the war, as part of the Marshall Aid Plan, it had been rebuilt and re-equipped by the US with top level and state-of-the-art production machinery. This produced a completely renewed industrial landscape, in marked contrast to the old and impoverished post-war conditions prevailing at many of the British factories in the Midlands and London. There was another highly visible legacy of the after effects of war on view. During my business dealings in Germany, I met a good number of industry officials, former veterans of the bitter fighting and carnage on the Eastern Front, who bore the horrific scars – disfigurement, lost limbs and maybe much more.

Yet, on another level, our close involvement with the Happich factory revealed to us a true microcosm of the booming industrial scene in post-war Germany. Once we had started to import their top quality hooding for the 280CE Mercedes convertible, it was only a matter of time before we were offering it as an expensive extra on our Ford convertibles. Its quality was immediately recognised in the car trade and soon we were doing good business selling to other car body builders and restorers. The hooding became one of those sideline ventures which consistently made money over the years.

*The Mercedes 600 Laundette completed*

# Chapter 9

# On a Knife-edge

Yet, as we discovered, success has both its challenges and drawbacks, certainly so in a field as fiercely competitive as ours and perhaps not as exposed to the same kind of public scrutiny of other commercial areas. Our ability to make a profit had become public knowledge – or at least available to public perusal – through the compulsory obligation to file the company accounts. The result: we became the target of various entrepreneurs, better described as 'con' men.

The activities of one of these characters almost brought our company to its knees. The gentleman concerned, although based in London, approached us with a request for the Argo franchise for Sweden, which would have given him the sole authority to import the vehicle into that territory. He declined our suggestion at the outset that he purchase a number of those vehicles, choosing to buy one only. However, we still decided to agree on his appointment, mainly because at the time we had no other interest from that region. After the initial purchase, he completely disappeared and was uncontactable. Months went by without any further orders and he failed to respond to our newsletters or correspondence. In short, we forgot about him and, legitimately – in our view – closed the file.

To our total surprise, some time later, we received the first of many solicitor's letters. We were accused of having offered the Argos directly to another potential agent in his territory, or so it was claimed, a year after having signed an agreement with him – and at discounted terms. Furthermore, he argued, this action had wrecked a major military contract he had been working on and cost him 'hundreds of thousands of pounds' in lost business. Even if the claims were unsustainable in a court of law, the costs involved to defend our case could have destroyed us financially.

On investigation, it would seem that an enquiry had indeed been received by us and a subsequent check had indicated that it was from 'dead' franchise territory. In fact, we should have been more careful and have contacted the original dealer we had appointed to confirm that he was not interested any longer. As a result, full dealer discount information had then been sent out to the enquirer. We were now in a dire predicament and facing a potentially business-destroying threat. The QC called in by our solicitor to advise us came up with a blunt and bleak response to my question as to how the case would stand up in court. Travelling up in the lift to his offices I asked him what he thought our chances were. 'Frankly, I would prefer to be acting for the other side', he told me.

We were being sued for a huge sum, one which would cost us the whole business and the freehold of our very valuable factory premises in Westerham. This would also bring with it the inevitable loss of our livelihood and attendant job losses; a sizeable blow, in fact, to the economy of a town the modest size of Westerham. Crucially, it would also have brought the production of Ford convertibles to an abrupt end. The stakes could not have been higher. Those were truly fraught times.

I spent many hours travelling back and forward to this businessman's office in London, literally begging him to let us off the hook. I recall trembling from head to foot with anxiety, standing outside his office. He had stitched us up, seemingly completely. He could even produce a copy of the army contract for hundreds of Argocats, together with the cancellation letter, when it was discovered we had offered the product to someone else. In short, it looked as if we had been 'nailed'.

Jeff was in despair. I too was almost beyond despair, the marketing being mainly my responsibility. And so this potential disaster came within my remit. But then, one extraordinary evening in a pub in Westerham, I fell into conversation with Rolley Atterbury, a friend in the printing trade, who – by sheer coincidence – was the previous owner of our factory building. I unburdened myself and told him the whole desperate story. To my amazement, he told me that there had been an individual circulating in the printing business, who had 'set up' people in a similar manner and then sued them, as we were threatened, for breach of contract. He mentioned the name of the 'businessman'. It was the same 'entrepreneur' who was posing such a threat to our own business.

A remarkable coincidence indeed! To have stumbled on this friend's story by accident. So we were in the hands of a professional scam operator. The very next day I contacted our solicitors. But, to my horror, they rolled out that routine phrase 'the law is the law'. However, they did suggest that, as there was evidence that he already had a record for this type of operation, it was unlikely that he would be keen to pursue his claim through the courts. Armed with this advice, that same morning I raised a banker's draft for £10,000 at Barclays, photocopied it and headed for London. Once in his office, I placed the photocopy of the draft on the 'businessman's' desk, along with a statement for him to sign, which effectively let us off the hook. I also showed him the original cheque in my wallet and presented him with an ultimatum: the cheque could be his, otherwise I would see him in court and I knew the history of his dealings – information that would make for interesting evidence. If he was going 'below the belt', then I would not hesitate to do the same.

It was an occasion which called for some bluff and strong nerve. I made it clear that, whatever the outcome of a court case, I would continue to watch his every move and that of his wife, whom I had already contacted. This was indeed true: before leaving my Westerham office earlier that same morning, I had tracked her down, via International Directory Enquiries. Not difficult to do, as she had an English surname and so was immediately traceable in the village where she lived near the edge of the Arctic Circle! I had no compunction in telling her just what her husband was doing to us and the information had clearly upset her. I told him this.

Confronted with this challenge, the 'entrepreneur' asked me to wait while he telephoned his lawyer. For ten long minutes I stood waiting in the corridor outside his office, tense and almost physically ill with worry. I can only imagine what transpired during that time, but presumably our 'con man' had owned up to a previous record of this kind of operation. I was called back into his office and he declared that he would accept the cheque and sign the prepared statement. Such relief – we were off the hook, but at a price, and not just a financial one. The stress of the episode affected my health and probably Jeff's as well. So it is with good reason that I will remember that office – and that man – for the rest of my life.

Unbelievably, we were to experience a similar 'set up', again, and in a remarkably similar manner. A Yorkshire businessman visited us to discuss the Argocat franchise for a certain area and bought two machines. We agreed to the deal and off he went. But, again, there was no follow-up response whatsoever.

We neither heard from him, nor received any requests for spare parts and accessories. It seemed strange to us at the time, but we gave it no further thought and in due course forgot about him.

Some while later, our secretary received a request from a garage in the north of England for Argocat literature. They asked whether, as car dealers, they could have a discount if they placed an immediate order for an Argocat. The literature was sent off, with no inkling of danger, along with price details.

Nothing more was heard for a while until, sure enough, out of the blue, a solicitor's letter arrived one morning. It detailed the substantial sum their client had spent travelling to research the whole project, how he'd bought a new Range Rover for towing purposes and spent money on PR, meetings etc. The principal accusation: we had broken the terms of the agreement by offering to supply within his territory – which was indeed true.

An error had occurred, there is no disputing that fact. Nowadays, with postcodes and computers to carry out detailed checks these errors can be avoided by setting up appropriate systems. But at that time – a mere thirty years ago, but a millennium ago in terms of technological developments – we were receiving enquiries from all over the world and couldn't even have begun to think about checking out each one in detail before replying. In any event, we were in serious trouble – yet again targets for a 'set-up' operation. How were we going to get out of this one?

I decided on a rescue plan rather on impulse and called the Yorkshire garage who had recently asked us for literature and dealer prices. Having never contacted them before myself, they were not familiar with my voice and I had a hunch I needed to follow through. Could the secretary who answered tell me how I might contact Mr. X as he had forgotten his AA map book in my office, which I wanted to return to him. To my astonishment, she replied: 'Oh, you mean Mrs ––'s husband. He comes in to see her from time to time. ' I'd stumbled across the link. Already things were falling into place: He had used his wife, who worked in the garage quite some distance away from where they lived, to originate the Argocat enquiry and lure us into the trap. Having uncovered the scam and how it was set up in one phone call, it was with some pleasure that I now dealt a telling blow.

I immediately called the 'con man' to tell him that I was sending up our foreman and an employee to collect the two vehicles I had supplied to him. I also informed him that he would be required to sign a disclaimer and that I would be prepared to go to court. Further, given the fact that we had certain information about his activities, I suggested that he might prefer to keep a low profile. I'd hit the nail on the head and he didn't put up a front or struggle, instead he backed off pretty quickly. He didn't know exactly what I had discovered, but clearly concluded that he couldn't take the risk either. We duly collected the vehicles and closed the book, with great relief, on yet another nasty episode.

No doubt there were individuals who sought to catch us out on other occasions, but Jeff and I managed to see most of the scams coming. And if one of us failed to smell the proverbial rat, the other one most certainly sniffed trouble a mile off. Experience was everything and certain patterns of approach became relatively easy to detect. In general, we followed the rule that the further a garage or individual was located from London, the more honest they or he would be, although admittedly the Yorkshire garage incident was an exception to this rule. Some enquirers, though, just inspired confidence, such was their sense of probity and fairness. For example, we would have trusted David Anderson and the Lovatt Estate operation near Inverness – who sold our vehicles for years – with anything. At times, they would owe us sums of £40,000 – £50,000 and at one difficult point – they had just installed a disastrous computer – they were unable to ascertain for months on end just what they owed us. But here a system of mutual trust was at work. One phone call to me, to check the outstanding balance on their account meant that the cheque would be in the post the next day.

In complete contrast, though, a London car dealer who tried to collect a Ford convertible without first paying was given very different treatment. The bruising experience of motor industry manufacturers had led to the accepted practice of purchasers being required to pay up before a vehicle left the factory gate. We followed the same principle in our own operation, a practice I had first encountered in the 1950s when working on vehicle delivery for my 'uncle' J. L.Wright at the Ford Dagenham plant during my university vacations. When we entered the factory at Dagenham at six or seven in the morning, we often carried bundles of cheques from dealers to whom deliveries had been made during the previous day or overnight. The accounts department insisted on having the cheques on their desk before the next day's batch of cars could be released. Not a bad system, but of course it was operating in the days long before direct debit transactions became the norm.

Years later, our own systems were still by no means perfect and it is true that our reluctance to put ourselves in the hands of what was then considered the 'dreaded' computer eventually made life rather complicated. Jeff had an instinctive distrust of anything that he couldn't check or use easily – and he was right. The accessing of information on spare parts was a good example of how our old method worked effectively. We were constantly being told that this kind of data should be held on a computer instead of a Cardex system. Yet the great advantage of the traditional Cardex file was that almost anyone who happened to be on duty on a Saturday morning could use it to refer to and consequently be of instant assistance to an unexpected customer.

The system worked like this: the customer would simply be taken over to the 'spares bin' and then pick out the card bearing the corresponding number and price. It was simplicity itself, a system which could be mastered by the average 14-year-old after, say, a day's experience of the process. Moreover, there was no risk of a total computer crash and the loss of a month's work. We were to learn about that experience in due course.

What did surprise us at the time, though, was the hugely effective role the computer could play in what was known as the model build variation, as operated by the leading car manufacturers. We had been accustomed to approaches in this area from Ford, Mercedes and others to build small quantities of special model variants. This was because their experimental and main production assembly line facilities could not cope with the disruption caused by this kind of specialised work.

The ultimate introduction of fully computerised 'build lines' resulted in quite the opposite effect: a remarkable degree of flexibility. Once a vehicle specification had been passed by the engineering department, its tool supplier lines cleared and the homogolation requirements checked and found to be in order, a red Escort convertible, for example, could in theory be built between a black two-door saloon and a white estate, and all with different engine options. This resulted in a degree of production adaptability absolutely unimaginable before the introduction of computerised systems to assembly line production.

On another front, however, there were grounds for despair with the emergence of Honda, Nissan and Toyota, all going from strength to strength, at the very same time as the British car industry slid steadily downhill. *Crayford* was the first company in Britain to exhibit the Japanese Subaru at the Earls Court Motor Show – in 1972 – following an approach by an Irish solicitor, who told us he had a model of the vehicle to display.

This strange little car arrived from the docks and I embarked on my usual waltz through the regulations to find a way to show it in the coachbuilding section of the show in West London. After some re-trimming of the roof panel it was duly slotted in. Jeff was by no means a so-called 'Jap-lover', the inelegant term used to describe those who over-enthused about the incoming products from Japan. This was an exception, he couldn't stop raving over the qualities of the Subaru. After many checks, he was in a state of pure disbelief at its economical petrol consumption and its attributes in general. Its motor was four cylinder horizontally opposed and, it was an off-white vehicle with a black leathercloth roof. We should have jumped at taking up the UK agency option for the Subaru there and then, but somehow – and sadly – we didn't.

These were testing times for us, inextricably linked as we were to the declining fortunes of the UK car industry. It was the steady fall in British exports which drove us, reluctantly, to be on the constant lookout for other products with potential outside the car world. The selling of sunbeds and wood-burning stoves was not something we had sought or wanted to be involved in, but it was a question of necessity – we were watching the gradual collapse of the industry we had relied on for developing our own business and making it a success.

The kind of experience our Spanish importer had to deal with only reflected the essence of the problem. He was selling our Capri convertibles and over a period of two years we shipped out quite a number to him in Madrid. Then he told us that his Spanish dealer clients had complained about the British built cars, on which we had constructed the convertible. In future, they said, they only wanted German chassis in a convertible. Other complications were also emerging. The dear little Mini, upon which we had based so many of our hopes in the early days turned out not to be a serious candidate for export success and, sadly, we received very few overseas orders for it.

Many of the complaints in those fraught days were around the products of sub-component suppliers. I recall one official in Canada telling us that the quality problems they experienced on the electrical side were such that Lucas, the British electrical component firm, for example, was jokingly known as 'The Prince of Darkness'! On one occasion, John Neil, the boss who transformed the famous Unipart business, when reporting in the *Financial Times* on the quality – or lack of it – in the early 1980s, stated: 'Our quality was so bad that only British Leyland would buy our parts'.

Taken all together, observations such as these, anecdotal or otherwise, amounted to a damaging indictment of British motor products of the day. At *Crayford* it was difficult for us to accept that the reputation of the UK, the country once known for having produced leading car and motorcycle products such as Humber Snipe and the Triumph Tiger, could sink so quickly and disastrously.

The problems we encountered with the Mini were symptomatic of the difficulties. The first Minis we received from the factory were – unbelievably – fitted with a piece of hanging wire which had to be pulled in order to open the door! The most primitive of door opening mechanisms and rightly condemned by Jeff as unacceptable. Yet years later, the same hanging wire mechanism was still in place, unmodified. Not only did it look dreadful, it was just that. Somehow, Britain could not get decent and acceptable products into the market place and we at *Crayford* suffered accordingly.

It was almost impossible, for instance, to acquire a good quality hood for a convertible. Home-based users had been accustomed to the veritable 'rag-top' approach. It was almost as if it was assumed that British owners derived some sort of perverse pleasure having to endure cold and soaking conditions whilst driving. A personal experience sums up the problem. At *Crayford* we were the owners of a beautiful MGB, which was in our second-hand car division. I decided one day to use it for a weekend visit to Plymouth, where our friends, the Mumfords, were then building the Marina convertible under licence. Maureen and I drove south west in steady rain and checked into the Holiday Inn. Memorably, it was there at the reception desk, when my wife Maureen turned and gave me a look that somehow said it all, one of those wordless moments, frozen in time and memory. We both looked as if we had been exposed to a wild, stormy night on our catamaran off Plymouth Sound.

We had travelled down from Kent with maps on our knees, not for navigational reasons, but to catch the water dripping from above. The reason: the hood of the MGB was totally unlined – and ugly to boot. It leaked and flapped, so much so that a travelling speed of 90 mph seemed like 150! Technically the hood was pathetic bearing in mind the model had been in volume production for years; also there was too much heat transfer through the firewall. So our feet fried. We were left to reflect ruefully that the car we'd left behind at home, an ordinary but trusty Ford Granada Ghia, would have delivered us down there in silence, warmth and comfort.

Hood manufacture in Britain was definitely a weak point. It was as if the British worker had never been trained to the required standard which satisfactory weatherproofing demanded. This was in such marked contrast to the experience with Germany where, perhaps, the severe winter weather in some areas had encouraged better development. They had thought it through properly and come up with a satisfactory product to solve the problems.

*Our Corsair Convertible, regarded by many as perhaps the most attractive Crayford convertible*

# Chapter 10

# Schnapps and Schubert

Finding a suitable hood for our convertibles presented a major problem for us, but eventually we heard about the Karl Deutsch firm in Cologne. They had been building convertibles – mainly Fords – since the early 1930s and clearly enjoyed a high reputation. There was even a local tradition, which pre-dated the war, where for ceremonies the mayor of the city was driven in a Deutsch convertible.

Jeff and I, together with our painter and close friend John Panther, decided to travel together in one of our Corsair convertibles to visit the Deutsch company's headquarters in Cologne – and it was a real eye-opener. Heading up the firm was Werner, the only one of the Deutsch sons to survive the war. He was neither a car fanatic nor an engineer, but he was building convertibles again and they were beautiful, equipped with an especially impressive hood. That visit marked a turning point, being the start of a long and immensely rewarding personal and business relationship. Werner loved this British connection. Ultimately, we were to market some of his cars as Crayford-Deutsch products.

We began our long collaboration by converting cars to the point where they needed the hood frames and canopy, at which point they were driven to Germany for completion work. Soon a system established itself: every few weeks, as Deutsch completed one or two of the vehicles, we would set off to Cologne with the next pair. There was only one problem – Werner's limitless hospitality! As each pleasurable weekend came to a close – and a generous amount of beer had been consumed – Jeff and I had to get into the two returning cars and head back through Germany and Belgium to the ferry. However, first we were expected to go through certain German traditions, which Werner, a charming businessman of the old school, insisted we follow. Before leaving, for instance, we were required to sit in his drawing-room and, with Frau Deutsch watching us closely, down a few schnapps to cement our good relationship with both the family and the company. Needless to say, there were times when this got a little out of hand. Werner would reach into the fridge for another bottle, while his wife, Eva, would head off to bed in a state of gentle exasperation. Then Jeff, who couldn't sing a note, would join me at our host's superb piano .... Cologne nights to remember, these – but they meant that we didn't head for home until the following morning and sometimes drove like madmen to catch the ferry.

The personal relationship with the family was to develop on several levels. Jeff soon discovered that Werner had a holiday house in the Eifel mountains, where there was good shooting – and even better food and wine – available. So he often headed off there on holiday and on one occasion my own daughter, Sarah, went over to stay with the Deutsch family for a while. The German influence made a deep impression on our family lives, even to the extent that, from early on, we adopted the seemingly indestructible matching lederhosen for our children. Made of tough hide and designed in such a way that they could be rolled down as the youngsters grew older and taller, to us these traditional knee-length breeches somehow epitomised German practicality and quality – products most assuredly made to last.

Amidst all this, it was instructive to discover at first hand just how cautiously and carefully a German company such as Deutsch developed a business relationship. For many years we addressed each other in the most formal way which is, indeed, usual even amongst Germans themselves. We were Mr and Mrs to them and so, rather against the grain, they had to be Herr and Frau for us. No question of moving over to calling each other by our Christian names. Not for many years, that is, until a surprising breakthrough about 5 years after we began dealing with each other. Werner had suggested that he and his old wartime friend, Franz Joseph (who spoke quite good English), together with Jeff and me, should visit a favourite local bar on the banks of the Rhine and it was there, during our beer and cheese session in Cologne, that Werner announced it was time to call each other by our first names. A most formal call for informality. Yet, for us, it marked an important step. We'd obviously earned this special honour and we drank to this newly conferred distinction quietly and respectfully. Yet, what a marked contrast this was to our relationships with American businessmen where, within minutes of a first meeting, everyone instantly used the 'Dick and Harry' form of familiarity.

The consolidation of our relationship with Deutsch gave us enormous business credibility in Germany and I am sure that when we came to negotiate 'factory approval endorsement' with Mercedes Benz for our estate car conversion, this long-standing association with one of the oldest German car firms was a crucial factor. Also the subsequent development of our Mercedes business in the early 1970s benefitted from the warranty arrangement. The Westerham-built all-new Mercedes Benz 'S' was launched as an estate in 1974. Some 15 of these expensive models were sold, including one direct order from Mercedes Benz – for the Italian screen star Sophia Loren, to transport her five pet dogs, presumably in the most eye-catching manner possible. This same model was also sold to wealthy clients in the US where it was built locally for us under licence by Harpers of Detroit.

The Mercedes-Benz connection was a huge boost to our business with conversion work referred to us by Mercedes Germany. I believe no other British car company enjoyed that benefit. As far as was humanly possible, we did everything according to the book. In the case of Deutsch, if the money we had transferred to cover the latest work ever failed to arrive, we were more upset than Werner.

One little known fact, in this context, is that at one point *Crayford* almost became a German company. At Werner's insistence we had gone over for a special chat. He told us then what we had been half expecting all along. He was no longer in good health and was thinking of retiring. Could we, he asked, work out a formula whereby we would take over the Deutsch factory and run it – possibly building the Mercedes estates in Cologne and the Ford versions in Britain?

The final plan we developed was to form a new company – *Crayford Deutsch* – in England and Germany, with Jeff based in Cologne as head of the whole engineering programme. It was indeed an alluring prospect. We both had the utmost respect for German car engineering and their scrupulous attention to detail appealed greatly to Jeff. His motto 'near enough is not good enough' had become a byword, encapsulating as it did an attitude which was wholly consistent with the spirit of the German approach. The financial ramifications of the proposed set-up were not explored in any detail but it was obvious that, above all, Werner was anxious to keep the name of Deutsch and he figured that the projected arrangement with us would be the best way of ensuring that would happen.

In all these dealings, there was a rewarding and mutual sense of understanding and, on reflection, it seems to me that of all the Europeans, the Germans were the people with whom we could do real business. In truth, they are so like us! Their reliability was second to none: if the discussion was about contract completion dates, when they looked you straight in the eye, saying 'we will do it', they did indeed mean just that. Whatever the project, they had thought it through carefully and at length and it would be completed satisfactorily, as initially agreed. It was an approach that inspired confidence and trust, whereas the same reassuring sense of reliability was not reflected in our many comparable business dealings in France, Spain or Italy.

The planned arrangement with Jeff working out of Cologne offered genuine possibilities. On a personal level, there was a further advantage. Jeff's wife, Mary, had a gift for languages and a natural flair for conversational German. Sadly, though, the Deutsch link-up was not to be. With regret, we had to give up on the plan due to a series of unforeseen developments. In the first instance, Werner's health was failing fast. There were other concerns as well arising from the prevailing financial climate. We were trading at 12 DM:£1 and became seriously worried when it strengthened to 10DM:£1. In these circumstances it seemed unlikely that our import of hooding material from the Happich company in Wuppertal and another source in Cologne, would or could withstand a price increase. Furthermore, it seemed to us that at ten to the pound value, the DM level would certainly damage the VW and Mercedes trade, but we were wrong as it turned out. The German capacity to control prices and yet maintain quality was outstanding – really impressive. The car products continued to stay competitive.

Finally, we received a call from Werner – he was having to close down the business and we were to order our last cars. So we agreed to send over a quantity of right-hand drive Ford Capris for eventual use on the British market. This signalled the end of our long relationship with Deutsch and it was a deeply sad day for us all. Werner subsequently passed away and the factory in Cologne was sold off. The distinguished name of Deutsch was to feature no more on German cars. But we remained in contact with his widow, Eva, who had always been so kind and hospitable to us.

*The Capri Convertible was a joint Crayford–Deutsch product which used the German hood system of excellent quality, but produced limited rear vision*

# Chapter 11

# Cologne Nights

There was so much to reflect upon and good times to recall from the Cologne connection – Jeff's attempts to grapple with the German language, most certainly. Whenever we were there, he always relied heavily upon my 'pidgin' German to deal with basic negotiations, even if some of those happened to occur in a night-club. Though ever the optimist, he was not an instinctively generous individual and he had been known even to attempt to turn his lack of German to advantage to keep down costs!

On one occasion in a club in Cologne, he decided that the evening was taking a boring turn and that some company was called for. I was then promptly despatched to the other end of the room to negotiate on his behalf with a certain hostess. Pressing a single pound note in my hand, he added: 'Do your best!'

Perhaps one of our most memorable, if alarming, experiences of Cologne good life occurred after we had sold the Cortina manufacturing rights for Belgium to a main Ford dealer in Brussels. To our surprise, the final payment was made in cash and we headed off to Germany carrying more money on our persons than was prudent. The following day found us celebrating in an exclusive, up-market Cologne club. I recall that it was located in a pedestrian precinct – and I do so for the simple reason that, when the trouble started, the police cars had difficulty gaining access to the scene.

All had gone smoothly until the early hours when Jeff declared that he was going upstairs with one of our friends to 'watch television'. At about 4.00 a.m. there was a knock on my door. It was Jeff, wearing nothing more than his vest. Visibly agitated and bedraggled, he announced that he'd run out of money and wanted to go home immediately. Chaos ensued. The girls told the management and the management called the police. In the midst of all this early morning mayhem, Jeff got dressed and walked downstairs into the dawn, just as the police were struggling to park their Opel Rekord patrol cars on the precinct pavement. As we walked quietly away from the club, now in turmoil, I challenged him: just how, I asked, had he managed to get rid of so much money in one night? He simply looked at me in that sheepish manner of his and patted his pocket!

Jeff's problems with the language had posed other difficulties – in our business dealings, to be precise, and he was acutely aware of that. It was clear that if we were to run Deutsch, as proposed, we would both have to learn German. Other difficulties loomed. In Germany, qualifications are a must, whatever trade you follow, and in that sense we were a little 'thin on the ground'. So, finally, it came as a great source of relief to learn that Jeff had decided to take German lessons, attending a course at the Berlitz Centre in Croydon. To my surprise, he seemed to be enjoying the tuition experience and had opted for two lessons a week. Yet, oddly, he declined to offer any tangible examples of his newly acquired linguistic skills. Eventually it transpired that the 'one-to-one' sessions with the young lady teacher were taking ever longer and had become the highlight of his week. The episode ended with Jeff giving up and abandoning all attempts to learn the language, despite an outlay of some hundreds of pounds in tuition fees.

The ultimate failure to link up with Deutsch, combined with the growing threat to our convertible monopoly meant that we had to redouble our efforts to diversify. They were many and varied and some I have now completely forgotten in the mists of time. To fill in the background, I have had to fall back on the enviable powers of recall of our good friend Colin Corke, one-time vicar of Tatsfield. It was Colin who reminded me that the Subaru, which we had shown at the Earls Court Motor Show in 1972, was in fact an off-white vehicle, with a black leathercloth roof. This is typical of Colin's attention to detail, a memory skill that is hugely impressive and, where Leyland products are concerned, positively encyclopaedic.

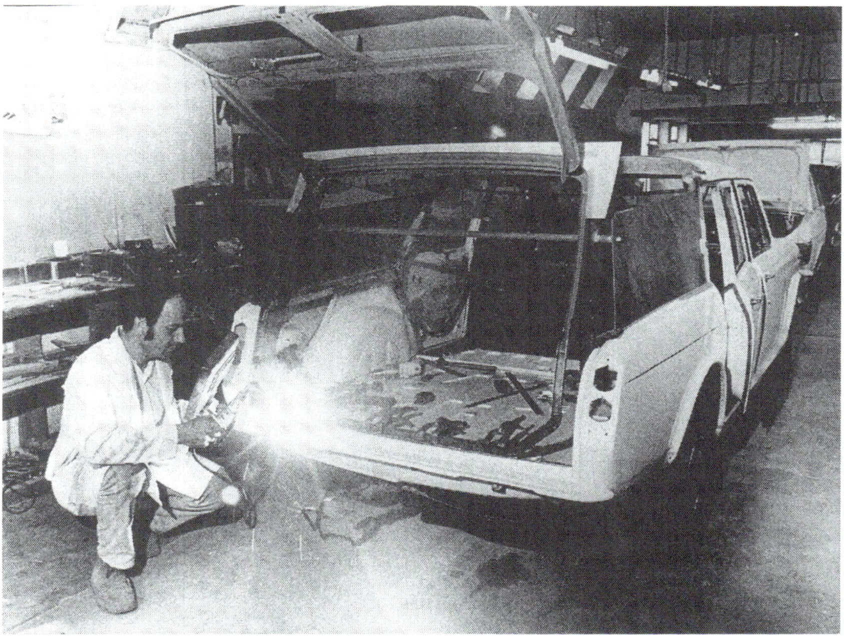

*Working on an Austin 3 litre Estate*

He reminded me once of the occasion when, during a train journey from Oxted to London for a diocesan conference, he found himself sitting opposite two car enthusiasts. The young men were deep in conversation about technical aspects of the *Crayford* BMC Estate cars (our BMC11/1300 version, which was launched in 1965). They were patently getting certain facts mixed up. To their astonishment, Colin politely interrupted their conversation and put them right immediately, gently pointing out just which models had been built and when. It must have been quite a shock to them, receiving such a flow of unsolicited expert information from a lone cleric, travelling with his ecclesiastical regalia.

# Chapter 12

# Our Man in Madrid

Francis Alcaraz first walked into our lives – and on to our *Crayford* stand at the Earls Court Motor Show – in the mid 60s. His overall bearing, sleek black hair and the unmistakable whiff of Spanish aftershave instantly marked him out as a charismatic and exotic figure. Our Man in Madrid, as he familiarly became known to us, was a supremely confident Tarzan-like figure. He spoke faultless English and impressed everyone.

He became a close friend of both our families. As an agent and distributor for our operations in Spain (by 1975 our biggest export market), he was also a source of much frustration as much because of the world and culture he represented, perhaps, as the cavalier, yet undoubtedly endearing, side of his personality.

The chief problem was the issue concerning how best to draw up his order to an exact or agreed format which allowed us an adequate time frame in which to build the required number of cars for export to Spain. A totally one-off ordering pattern had developed and this at an impossibly late stage in the negotiations. Francis would regularly turn up at my home in Kent, direct by taxi from Heathrow, carrying no luggage other than a small briefcase from which he would pull out a plastic carrier bag stuffed with Pesetas. His instructions were remarkably short on detail.

'That's the deposit', he would say. 'I want five of this and five of that.' Such was, in essence, his ordering method, making no allowance for the fact that we, in turn, had to work to a strict ordering pattern to fit in with our own suppliers' schedules. We had to reserve the basic models from Ford six months in advance at the very least. To get a Spanish company to commit themselves on issues such as exact colour and model choices that far ahead – and in writing – proved to be virtually impossible. Interestingly, it is only now, having spent over 20 years in retirement living in Spain, that I begin to truly understand and appreciate the background to such haywire methods of negotiation.

At the time it was infuriating, to say the least. Because of import restrictions imposed Francis could only get import licences for five models of each type of car at a time. And even then this inevitably called for a high degree of careful adaptation and juggling to get round all the red tape. Nonetheless, we were able to present vehicles at the Barcelona Motor Show for many years – our most favourite of all the European motor shows. It was in Barcelona that we first presented to the public our Mercedes estate and went on to win the gold medal award in 1974.

It is curious how typically laid back this show was. There seemed to be no sense of real urgency. One recollection remains vivid, being somehow symptomatic of what went on there at the time. It was press opening day and there were two grey German transporters parked in the road outside with some of the show cars still waiting to be offloaded. Inside the show arena, the truck drivers in their overalls were partying on the still empty Mercedes and BMW stands. That little scene seemed to sum up the idiosyncratic, if joyous, Spanish way of business life.

There were other hurdles to be regularly surmounted:

lubricating your progress through the path of officialdom (otherwise known as bribery and corruption) was part and parcel of Spanish life. Amongst the other outlets pursued by our agent, Francis Alcaraz, was the importing of Scotch whisky – often a felicitous aid to smoothing our path. Serious difficulties encountered crossing the Spanish frontier with our vehicles on one occasion, for instance, meant a long wait whilst the necessary crates of whisky were transferred from one customs office to another, presumably destined for Madrid. This was a regular occurrence, with us finally being waved through with great gusto after, that is, the necessary and vital matter of 'lubrication' had been sorted out. Spirits truly oiled the wheels. I remember when Alcaraz arranged for four crates of whisky to be delivered to Jeff's home and mine, the liquor was a straight, if unexplained, gift. That summed up Spain and also what our Man in Madrid was all about. Yet, he would have been offended had we refused his gift. He was well liked by our family. The children loved his visits and his tales about 'bull meat sandwiches' . But he had his moments: he caused great horror and consternation when he picked up their much loved pet pussycat by the tail and swung it around in the air several times, before dropping the terrified animal!

The man was as generous as he was unpredictable. The returns from him came in many guises, sometimes even in the unlikely form of new Ford engines. If we 're-engined', say, 15 new cars with V6 or V8 motors for the Spanish market, the originals taken out of the vehicles became available to us. Jeff and I frequently found ourselves confronted with a row of gleaming new engines, which had never come into either the accountancy or tax calculations. By default almost, these became an invaluable extra source of revenue to meet family school fees.

The truth was that there were no limits to Francis's generosity towards us. At one point, we needed our catamaran delivered on its trailer from Kent to Javea, near Alicante. He arranged for it to be collected from the Bilbao ferry and towed all the way down to Javea at no cost. As another instance of this, after one of the Barcelona Motor Shows, my wife, Maureen took a short break by travelling to Madrid on the famous 'Talgo' high-speed express train. Arriving late at night in the city, having failed to talk her out of such a lone adventure, Francis promptly flew down in time to be on the platform to meet her to make sure she was ok and entertain her over dinner. The fact that the station restaurant was by that time closed left him undeterred. He caused a big fuss and finally managed to pressure the management into re-opening, just for the two of them.

Despite his natural charm, his dealings in Germany were not altogether a success. We had introduced him to our good friend Werner Deutsch.They did do some work together, but the Germans just could not cope with his haphazard Spanish way of going about his business – especially the almost zero response to any correspondence sent to him. Predictably, perhaps, a strange development occurred after our great friend and enigmatic traveller-business associate, Francis, had alas died in the early 1980s. It happened like this: some six months had elapsed following his death, when we received a call from Werner in Cologne. His friend and owner of an underground car park in Cologne had discovered a row of new, unclaimed Mercedes which had accumulated a huge bill in parking fees. The vehicles had been parked there by Francis the previous year. It eventually transpired that he had been suffering from a severe illness affecting the brain and become uncharacteristically forgetful. Nieves, his secretary and partner in Madrid, confirmed that he had some cars in Germany and, sure enough, the vehicles in that Cologne car park matched the descriptions.

This was to present us with quite a dilemma: expensive cars without any paperwork, no number plates and no proven title of ownership. Armed with a lot of cash, Jeff and I travelled to

Cologne to try and sort it out. We did manage, with Werner's help. To minimise the death duties accruing on Francis's estate, we set about turning these left-hand drive vehicles into money, fitting them first with English trade plates and driving them back in convoy to the UK, and predictably into the arms of over-officious customs officers at Dover.

We turned one of the models into the Condor – an SLC station wagon, using the glass back door that Triplex, I believe, had styled for one of the British Leyland Princess prototypes. Another was the celebrated yellow model which we bullet-proofed and ultimately sold to the mystery client in Mexico City. The proceeds from these sales were passed on to Nieves. The other vehicles were all sold in various ways. We persuaded Nieves to travel over to England, as we had money placed in a Croydon bank for her. The cash input was clearly welcome. Francis had left his financial affairs in a state of some confusion – no doubt arising from his illness, although it had always seemed to me that he had run his entire life out of a small pocket notebook. There were almost certainly other unclaimed cars parked in garages elsewhere in Europe. One story came to my attention which suggested a similar pattern: a number of Lotus cars, equally unclaimed, parked 'somewhere' again in Europe. They would almost certainly have been his, but were never traced.

There is one special landmark in Spain, which strongly reminds me of him – a man I still miss. The location is near Javea – my home since retirement in 1987 – not far from the villa which served as our office from 1972, and for which the British Treasury had given their authority to purchase as such because of our substantial export trade to Spain. The site which triggers a memorable incident lies north of Alicante on the N332. Here, on the hard shoulder, he decided with his typical flair and impetuosity to overtake – at around 60 mph and on the wrong side of a long stationary traffic queue. The Guardia, however, were waiting and stepped out to flag us down. Francis promptly gave them so much abuse, all delivered in his impeccably upper class Castilian accent that, much to my relief and astonishment, they let him go. Again, that was Francis – it was also Spain.

# Chapter 13

# ATV and Polecat

The Argo business started with the Amphicat which Francis Alcaraz had been importing into Spain from Beehoo Industries near Toronto. We first saw it on the Albion stand at the Barcelona Show. As Geoff and I were both avid off-road motorcyclists, the concept of a six-wheel drive, lightweight, cross country vehicle appealed, so we borrowed it and displayed it on our own stand at the Earls Court Show in the mid-seventies, which resulted in some strong enquiries. We therefore returned the machine back to Spain and I went to Canada to see Ronnie Beehoo and acquire the agency for Britain. When the first delivery arrived we invited David Anderson of Aird Motors, Beauly to come down and try one out with a view to Aird Motors taking the agency for Scotland. He had already seen it on our stand at the Earls Court Motor Show and we thought this company would be ideal, being part of the Lovatt Estate, which had enormous influence in Scotland. They also had the capital to finance an agency of this type. Near the works in Westerham, there was an excellent test area with a small lake and steep climb. On that first day, Jeffrey and I knew immediately that David Anderson had exceptional driving skill. Aird Motors was to become our best agent in Europe and David Anderson a close personal friend.

Unfortunately, the Amphicat reliability was so poor that breakdowns were frequent. Amongst other items, the ignition switch (which I think was British – the Canadians told us it was made by 'Lucus Prince of Darkness' in the UK, such was the reputation of British electrics!) would let in rain water, this resulted in the engine starting and if the machine, which had automatic transmission, had been left in gear it would head off on its own! Apparently one of them headed off on its own out of the work's car park near Toronto, crossed the road, mounted the pavement and crashed through the window of a car show room!

*Inside the Argocat ATV storeroom at the Westerham factory*

By sheer coincidence, I somehow heard of the Argo which was being built by Ontario Drive and Gear just down the road from Beehoo, in a place called New Hamburg. The Argo was a superior machine, mainly because the company was German owned and they concentrated mainly on machining, so their quality control was good; also they produced an eight-wheeler which was, in due course, to dominate the market. We took an enormous financial gamble and ordered four eight-wheelers direct from ODG. Aird Motors took two of them fairly quickly. Crayford started to carry out modifications and improvements from an early date as the Argo had its own problems to begin with, a bit like the Amphicat. The axles where too thin and the front axles bent easily when the vehicle hit a boulder on a downhill run. The worst problem in the early years was the gear box and its input shaft. The Argo used a skid steer system which relied on the transmission to one side being slowed by a disc and power bled to the other via a differential, which put enormous strain on the gearbox's internals.

Before long we had over 100 eight-wheelers operating in Scotland and the North of England. David Anderson would phone me at home at least once a week, probably with a glass of whisky in hand, to ask for an enormous list of spares and with a request for free warranty replacement parts. Several times we almost ran out of gear box parts during the late 1970s and on a number of occasions I personally flew to Canada, with virtually no luggage so that I could return laden with gear box spares.

The Argo business grew steadily and filled the need that we had always had for a winter product. Convertibles were hard to sell in the winter, though we had actually managed to persuade Norris Lawley and his boss Harry Cressman at Bristol Street Motors in Birmingham to take two cars a week for stock, even if it was snowing!

One problem we did find in converting cars which were not immediately used – inventory stock building as it is sometimes called – was that there is no immediate feedback from customers and this can be something of a problem whilst you are in constant run production. For example, if dealers stored cars for us right through the winter months and then started selling in February or March we would only then, of course, find out what mistakes had been made in the previous November or December production. We were not alone in this: the major manufacturers suffered from a similar problem when building, say, 800 Ford Fiestas a week and starting to stockpile for inventory during a slack period. Only when 2-3,000 cars are released onto the market in a later month, do they discover that the operator assembling a particular component was having a bad few days and a warranty nightmare develops, or even a major recall. Our problems were not quite of that magnitude, but nevertheless fairly severe, particularly if cars had been stored during the winter months, sitting under two feet of snow for a few weeks, as indeed happened to us on one occasion.

In any event, the Argo filled this winter space and continued to grow in sales. We were probably the ideal agency for ODG, not too big and prepared to get our hands dirty. You had to be with the Argo, because it would get to places that virtually no other vehicle could reach and if it broke down in that situation you had to fix it there and then. Nobody could help you unless they had another Argo available. With its very low ground pressure (about 4psi), it travelled easily with tracks on top of deep powdered snow, an impossible feat with most other vehicles. Having a low centre of gravity, it could also cross frighteningly steep gradients and finally swim across lakes and rivers. We used to say to a potential dealer: if you can succeed in following the Argo with any other type of vehicle for a few hours, then we will give you one free! We never ever had a single challenge on this one, quite a credit to the Argo. With our experience in off-road work, Jeffrey and I eventually persuaded ODG to give us a huge marketing territory, covering most of Europe and one or two other overseas territories. But, at the same time we became uneasy about the possibility of a sudden supply stoppage from Canada, should something unforeseen go seriously wrong. So we started to develop our own contingency plans.

As the Argo developed into our main earner we realized how vulnerable we were, either to unexpected competition from a similar product or the cessation of production in Hamburg. We therefore worked on an extended secret programme to cover these eventualities. First I went to the USA and in less than three weeks visited all the North American manufacturers of any similar product. I used a cheap ten-day roving airline ticket and my plan was to find out if there was a serious competitor, who could suddenly be importing into Europe and confront us. I found nothing of equal quality, with the engineering skill and capacity of ODG, so this was time well spent. Whilst on this trip I also made some unannounced visits to a couple of Argo distributors. This proved really useful and I remained in close contact with several of them for many years, especially the dealer in Edmonton, Alberta who also became a friend.

The second part of our plan to protect our position was a secret development programme of a different body type with our own moulding and a diesel engine installation. There were other special parts that we might also put into production on our own, enabling us to manufacture the entire vehicle fairly quickly. To find an alternative gear box and transmission layout would have been a real problem, but it could be done. At this time. I was also slightly uneasy about the early appearance of the Japanese built four-wheel cross-country vehicles called Quads, built by Honda and others, using transmission layouts which could easily be adapted for six- or eight-wheel vehicles such as the Argo. We had the odd panic moment when a competitor raised its head in Europe. A firm near Edinburgh, for instance, started producing an eight-wheeler, another one also appeared in France. I already knew that the French were trying hard when I went out to Iraq in 1984 to demonstrate the Argo to the Iraqi army, who wanted to use them for launching Swingfire Missiles. They were always very pro-British and liked to use British equipment because of their close historic relationship with the British army. I went to the swamps near

Basra to give my two day demonstration – in the deep mud. Near the entry point of the swamps where we did our testing and demonstrating for the army and demonstrating, there were fairly fresh track marks which I recognized to be those of the French machine. I have often thought of those officers and their subordinates. They were easy to work with. The British army had a huge influence there and one of the largest British bases in the world had been in Iraq. The sergeant I worked with a lot had just one word of English: when we solved a problem of some sort, he would give me a little salute saying 'smashing!' After a really tough day's work on the edge of the swamp, one of the officers would back up his Range Rover and we would all have a Pepsi – of course no alcohol was allowed. The officers looked very British in their uniforms, and a number of them spoke English with a distinctly public school accent! I remember asking one of them if I could see his hat. It was made by Bates of London, the same company that made my father's RAF Officer's cap which he passed on to me on to me after the war and I had used during my National Service.

With a huge potential market, the Argo was to take us to many places around the world. I demonstrated from Helsinki in Finland to Jerez de la Frontera in Spain. The constant marketing effort, combined with regular visits to the factory in Canada and the maintaining of good relations with ODG kept the product at the forefront of its class. In later years, the introduction of the Japanese Quad had us slightly worried, as previously mentioned, but it did not have the load capacity of the Argo nor did it have the amphibious or soft snow ability. Perhaps this is why it is still being manufactured today. Secretly I was much more worried about its transmission layout and the Japanese build quality, which is legendary. Many of the components could easily be adapted for use in an all-terrain vehicle (ATV). Eventually the inevitable happened, I heard of a six-wheeler going into production in western Japan. I flew out there and visited the factory. I was astonished to watch the sales manager of the small engineering company start the machine, get out and then give a complete demonstration using a digital radio remote control system. However, I did not feel they represented a threat, although I did spot parked outside an agricultural machinery supplier, a new eight-wheel vehicle which certainly could be a competitor, made by the engineering giant Mitsubishi. In order to control the possibility of this becoming a competitor, we took on the franchise for the machine for Britain, calling it the Hillfarmer. To avoid upsetting our colleagues at ODG in Canada, we set up a separate office in Oxted in Surrey and registered a company to market the machine.

We sold a small trickle of these machines, but found dealing with the Mitsubishi organization a nightmare. They took weeks to deal with anything and the spare supply situation was agonizingly slow. With the Argo on the other hand, if I had a real problem I could phone Bob Archer the sales manager at ODG and he would do everything humanly possible to help, even though it was not strictly his job. Problems came and went in our relationship with ODG, but somehow Bob Archer always calmed things down and a long-term friendship built up. His dry sense of humour was a help. It is not related to Argo but I cannot forget an occasion when I took him to the muddy, smelly, dirty creek near Faversham in Kent where I kept a Snow Goose catamaran. The tide was out, it was drizzling with rain and the yachts were sitting on the filthy, smelly mud, some of them tipped over on their sides. The landscape all around us was boringly flat marshland. Bob looked down at the mud in the creek, with a small trickle of greenish-brown water still running out, and with raised eyebrows just said: 'You go sailing here?' When he had a point he knew how to make it without being offensive. In comparison with my experience of sailing in Canada in those beautifully clean lakes with immaculate marinas and excellent organization, the British muddy creek is a different concept.

The Mitsubishi Hillfarmer finally proved too much for us, because of difficult relationships with the factory in Japan. We had been corresponding with a Mr Wanamoto about spares and other problems and seldom getting a reply. If it did come at all, it was usually two or three weeks late. It was only when I attended a meeting at the factory in Japan to try to sort out our problems that they pointed out that they had several hundred Wanamoto's in various departments! The size of the Mitsubishi Corporation, who are also well-established shipbuilders and aircraft manufacturers, is staggering. The taxis we used in Tokyo were often Mitsubishi, even the lift in my hotel and the TV in the bedroom had the Mitsubishi logo. The little Hillfarmer eight-wheel drive tractor, however, was typical of many Japanese products. Most of it was made by relatively small companies, who manufactured sub-assemblies as some of the products are built ex-factory. In the same way perhaps as the Ford Cortina convertibles were, in fact, made by *Crayford.* Towards the end, I almost gave up trying to get a sensible spare supply service from the main factory and instead found a helpful Mitsubishi agency near Tokyo, who would actually get things dispatched.

However, we still continued to order some parts, but 'the last straw' came when we were phoned by the freight office at Heathrow Airport in London, asking us to collect a crate of spare parts. This involved a man with a truck for nearly a whole day and a horrific airfreight bill from Japan. The long wooden box tube, when it arrived, was about six inches by six inches and ten feet long. It took us completely by surprise. We opened it only to find the Japanese had sent us a piece of ordinary Bundy brake line pipe that is easily and normally supplied in a coil. I can not only still see Jeffrey's face, but also still hear the language!

There and then, we decided that enough was enough and that was the end of the problem as far as we were concerned. We found certain aspects of our Japanese partner's management totally incomprehensible and impossibly difficult to work with. If one was unkind, one could describe it as stupidity as much as anything, but it is just a cultural difference and very often a result of a communication problem. In any event, the Hillfarmer from Mitsubishi had not turned out to be such a serious threat after all. Being of all-steel construction, the ground pressure was far too high because of its weight and it could not really compete with the Argo, so that project ended.

Other off-road vehicles that we built, examined, tested or purchased included an American four-wheel crop sprayer with incredible ground clearance. The Argo had some success as a sprayer, because of its low ground pressure and we thought that this American product might follow on. However, as with some other American products we had looked at, the build quality was a bit suspect. ODG produced a three-wheeler off-road motorbike to compete with the early Japanese motorized three-wheelers, which farmers had started to purchase in some quantity. I was invited over to Canada to the product launch at the factory and then, at the last minute, was asked to give the demonstration ride on the new machine, in front of all the dealers from Canada and America as well as various assembled guests. I had to carry out this demonstration outside the factory, on really steep slopes with transverse gradients, which can pose problems on a three wheel motorcycle. In addition to this, I had never ridden a three-wheeler cross-country motorcycle in my life. I can still clearly recall the first time I tried a steep descent in front of the assembled crowd, having had virtually no time at all to practice. Thank heavens for those many years spent in British motorcycle off-road events. The reason why ODG chose me was that they did not have any bikers on the staff, so I was the next best thing. It was a heart-stopping experience which I will never forget!

During my travels in the United States I had seen a strange, small, steel, four-wheel drive, off-road vehicle which consisted of nothing more than two large steel boxes, linked with a central lateral pivot with two wheels on each box. This simplicity meant that suspension was not essential and the rock climbing ability was exceptional. We built a similar machine and it was the only time I can remember that we ever produced a vehicle or conversion which was based on another product. Many of our ideas originated in The Ship, our local pub in Tatsfield, with quick designs sketched out on the back of a beer mat. We used to meet there on a Wednesday or Friday evening for a drink with John Panther and other friends. Sometimes, after a few beers during the evening, we would then drive along Chestnut Avenue where Jeffrey lived, for a last drink in Biggin Hill. This leafy, dark avenue was frequently used at night by lovers, who had locked themselves in their cars. A favourite naughty trick played by John was to pull up our long wheelbase Land Rover alongside such a car, open the window, lean down and thump on the car roof. The perplexed and perhaps partially dressed male would wind down his window to find out what we wanted, only to be asked if he knew the way to Biggin Hill!

The design for the Polecat started with a sketch on a beermat. We decided to produce it in time for the annual Earls Court Show, so it had to be designed and the prototype manufactured in a rush. The plan was to produce the permanent four-wheel drive vehicle in steel rather than ABS or GRP, as we had regularly run into opposition to any form of plastic when dealing with the military. Any army workshop can repair steel vehicles in almost any location in the world using standard welding equipment, but vacuum or static plastic moulded bodies are quite a different matter. Jeffrey drew the basic body shell with a wheel arch clearance that allowed us to use the full range of Land Rover wheel and tyre types, which are also frequently used by the military and some agricultural departments.

A few days before the show, we had a panic phone call late at night from one of our sub-contractors, Eric Moss, who was something of a loner, typical of the sort of people we have in Britain. He lived down a muddy lane in Tatsfield and had quite exceptional talent. We had given him the weekend job of building the body shell. He phoned Jeffrey with a crisis message: the measurements must somehow be wrong, as the vehicle body shell was nearly finished and there was no space in the wheel arch for a normal wheel, let alone a Land Rover wheel or a balloon tyre. It transpired that there was some confusion, because a small dot had not reproduced on the photocopy of the drawing. I think Jeffrey had drawn two foot eleven inches and it came out as only one foot eleven inches. I can't be sure that this was the problem and I wish I really knew. But I strongly suspect that, in fact, there was some confusion between imperial and metric measurements, as at that time we were right in the middle of the changeover and because of this we were experiencing problems almost daily. However, luckily, the result was a bonus. I had often heard people say that 'The skill in successful business is when you turn a potential disaster into a benefit'. Sometimes you can indeed do just that, as we did on this occasion. Eric ran a cutter right round the entire body shell, in effect tri-panning the vehicle halfway down the side wall. Then we welded in a massive, folded, sixteen gauge top hat section, to give the vehicle the lift that was needed for wheel arch clearance. In fact, it suited the vehicle very well and on the show stand at Earls Court, a number of wise and knowledgeable people congratulated us on this sensible strengthening feature. Little did they know!

The Polecat produced several famous occasions in the *Crayford* history. When it was completed, just a few days before the launch at the 1971 Motor Show, the men all gathered at the main door of the works in Westerham to watch me head off at some speed down the A25 in the direction of Oxted. There is a right hand bend, where I would normally swing left into a small lane that led to our test site; a field where there was mud and water. However, as I turned the steering wheel to the left the lack of front-to-rear and side-to-side differential came into play, the vehicle understeered violently and careered straight on into the rear of a parked car, causing extensive damage to the car, yet almost none to the Polecat. I did a very slow about-turn and dejected, headed back to the works where the men were waiting – some in dismay, others with a grin. I jumped out of the machine, which we towed into the works and I walked off in the direction of the solicitor's office on the corner, to make my apologies and sort out the damage to the car. But the car had gone. I went in and explained the situation and asked who owned the blue Triumph I had hit half an hour previously. They knew absolutely nothing about the car nor the accident and so I left totally bewildered. Some unfortunate would return to discover the back of his car had been savaged and no doubt turn up in a few days' time, when we would hear all about it. Mysteriously, though, we never did hear a thing and could do nothing to find the person whose car had been damaged.

The next Polecat lesson also took place on the A25. We had it loaded on a trailer and were leaving Oxted, when we had to slow down slightly. To our horror the Polecat, which had somehow become detached from its securing chain, had jumped off the trailer! It overtook us at speed on the right hand side of the road and we watched it hurtle past us, straight into the front of an oncoming Ford, with a full family on board! They were shaken and very cross, as anyone would be when a strange, driverless vehicle comes at you on the wrong side of the road and crashes into the front of your car! Luckily, we were not far from the *Crayford* works in Westerham and so we lent them a car and kept theirs to fix it. With heavy heart now, Jeffrey and I headed off again to a lake at East Grinstead, where we were to give a demonstration of the Polecat's amphibious

*Jeff Smith with Polecat on the front cover*
The South African Engineer

ability to a potential buyer of the project. Unfortunately, when the Polecat had jumped off its trailer at Oxted and hit the road with stationary wheels, the shock load had severed the key in the rear drive transmission to the wheels. When we got to the lake we had the embarrassing job of explaining all this to the gentleman, who was seriously thinking of buying the project from us – drawings, tooling, manufacturing, licence the lot. To our surprise and delight and perhaps typical of a Northerner, he agreed to take off his jacket, get stuck in and help us push the vehicle into the lake to see the water jet perform. Then we had to tow it out. He put his smart jacket back on, got into his new Aston Martin and simply said: 'Yes it seems to be a great machine, don't worry about your accident.' He was a real no-nonsense man and we appreciated his attitude. Off he went and eventually a deal was done.

There had been some serious enquiries from South Africa, where they hoped to build the Polecat under licence and in fact it even featured on the front cover of a South African military equipment magazine. But by then we had decided to sell . It had become obvious to us by that stage in the *Crayford* development, that our expertise lay largely in the ability to identify a need, put the package together with a prototype and then sell the entire project. The Polecat as a product never got off the ground and into volume production, but the concept of rugged simplicity was, I am sure, the right one.

Many years later, working as a 'retired' engineer for Oxfam in many different third world countries, I often longed for a simple, unbreakable, slow ATV for my work around the refugee camps. In a Rwandan camp, I once had the water and engineering supply responsibility for 350,000 people. My staff and I were driving around all day long in heavy, expensive Land Rovers and Land Cruisers, which had the disadvantage of high potential speed, which meant that if I sent the driver off on an errand, he might disappear through the camp in a cloud of dust at 50mph or more. Speed related accidents are common with African drivers. A simple vehicle like the Polecat would have cost only a fraction to run and have been less likely to participate in the 'going home' Grand Prix, which is sometimes the evening fun for aid workers and their drivers.

Sometimes I look at the reliable, simple, diesel engine dump trucks on building sites and think how suitable that platform would be, if re-engineered to carry out the rugged duty for which the Polecat was intended. Although, of course, they would not have the amphibious capability. The Polecat prototype was finally loaded onto our huge trailer, complete with jigs, tooling and a complete 'build manual'. Jeffrey and I delivered our project to a hotel in the north of England where the new owner and his son were staying. We collected our cheque and left. Curiously, we were to hear no more about the product and it never appeared in public that we heard of. In one sense we were eating our own seed corn. We developed a product, used our extensive engineering experience and ideas to make it work, drew it, tooled it and then when it was just about ready to go into production – when it might easily have run for ten years making a considerable contribution to *Crayford* annual income – we sold it for a lump sum.

We had discovered by then that although the rewards of a constant production run were great, so also were the headaches. More and more, the public was learning to take legal action against any product that it thought was not performing adequately and we had some frightening moments. On one occasion a convertible hood had ripped off a *Crayford* Cortina at speed and wrapped itself around the head of a following motorcyclist. He was lucky not to be killed and we were lucky not to be sued. On another occasion, for some reason we never understood, a tailgate fell off the back of one of our BMC 1100 estates and caused mayhem amongst the following traffic. One problem we always had to keep an eye out for, which could end in such disasters, was the possibility that no one had thought of telling you that three months previously

– or whenever – a local garage had removed the tail gate or the roof for a repair of some sort and not replaced it correctly. This was always a dangerous problem. True off-road vehicles, such as the Argo and the Polecat, were a potential litigation nightmare and seldom a winter passed without a 'near-death' experience occurring. There were one or two occasions when, because of the very nature of an amphibious vehicle, the floor would fill with petrol fumes, as the under tray was totally sealed and when the ignition key was turned there would be a mighty explosion. One such unfortunate driver was blown clean out of the vehicle some ten to fifteen feet.

On another occasion, a day or so after his new Argo had been delivered, the new owner took it out for a demonstration run in front of his family up in the mountains, somewhere in Germany, and killed himself within a few minutes. The public were slow to learn that with an amphibious vehicle the body, or hull as we called it, must obviously be watertight. This was an enormous disadvantage where fuel and fume build-up was concerned. With a car or any normal motor vehicle, any drip from the fuel system or gas build-up is very unlikely, as the under tray of the vehicle is open. With an Argo or amphibious vehicle, as with a boat, the fire or explosion potential is considerable.

However, the vast majority of our accidents were without serious injury and some even producing mirth. A driver crossing a frozen lake climbed out of his Argo to help his dog back into the vehicle, only to fall straight through the ice himself, because both the dog and the Argo had a lower ground pressure than he did. A human being has, in fact, quite a high ground pressure, about eight to ten pounds per square inch.

A more serious type of accident occurred when I was selling the company in 1987, two years after Jeffrey's death. Three Irishmen had heard of the possible sale of the business and came over to Westerham. I took them for a demonstration ride and used a six-wheeler, only because it happened to be available. Normally, I would have used the eight-wheeler which was longer and more stable. I chose the short, steep slopes along the side of Chestnut Avenue in Tatsfield and on climbing one of these semi-vertical slopes, the Argo did what tanks sometimes do, it climbed to a near-vertical point, where the vehicle finally rolled over backwards. Thank goodness the three Irish visitors were thrown out. I was not, however, and one of my legs somehow got trapped behind a control lever. The leg refused to break, but I was very badly hurt and the bruise is still with me. We were all shaken, but managed to drive the Land Rover back to the factory and discussed our lucky escape over a cup of tea. One of the party was really badly shaken and so I went into the outer office and asked Maureen to check him over to make sure no damage was done. I must say, the Irish took their 'near-death' experience in good spirit. In years to come, I expect it made a good yarn back home. Their plan had been to transfer *Crayford* – lock, stock and barrel – to Belfast, where there were engineering skills available and considerable tax benefits.

Belfast, in fact, had a long history as one of Britain's largest engineering facilities and as home to some of her largest shipyards and aircraft manufacturers. In other words, they had planned to do a sort of De Lorean deal, but nothing came of it. We did, however, become quite good friends despite their fright and would joke on the phone from time to time. On the other hand, the subject of a transfer did not go down too well with my staff. I can remember when they had obviously 'got wind' of what was going on. I went into the canteen and suggested to two or three of them that they might like to do a year's handover work, training staff in Belfast. They looked at me as if I had completely lost my mind and my foreman let out a string of muted obscenities! This was at a time when Northern Ireland was a scene of almost permanent murder and terrorist activities. I could have had a problem there. As it happened, the Irish project did not go forward. I soon realised that an engineering firm based near London, with freehold premises, no mortgage or debts and a long profit history would quickly find a buyer.

## Chapter 14

# Crayford and Motorbikes

A mutual interest in motorcycles was what originally brought Jeff and me together and that shared passion was a constant throughout our *Crayford* years. This 'biker' interest was also pursued equally passionately by my own two sons, Sean and Peter and, maybe surprisingly, daughter Sarah.

Peter Agg, the managing director at Lambretta Trojan, had first engaged me – back in 1960 – precisely because of my experience on two wheels. The motorcycling influence at Lambretta was strong in those formative days. Both the chief engineer, Ian Williams, and Jeff – the talented technician brought over from Wales as leading engineer in the Experimental Department – had similar backgrounds. So, it was no surprise then that Peter Agg took Lambretta to the top of the UK motorcycle sales league. As assistant sales manager I watched in admiration as he built up a hugely profitable business, based on an imported scooter, transported in vast numbers from Italy by train and sold in thousands in the UK. In fact, Britain was one of the very few countries in the world where our company outsold Vespa.

One particular incident stands out from those early days: we were the official 'company works' entry in a sidecar motorcross event and I was the unwilling, inexperienced and terrified sidecar passenger. Jeff was at the helm, riding powerfully and leading the field, when suddenly we sank in deep mud, in the midst of some thick bushes. Thankfully a big hand was there to help us out – in the powerful form of Ian Williams who managed to drag the whole outfit out of the mud, only for me to then tumble backwards over a log back into the mire – it was a scene reminiscent of a *Carry On* film. Further spills were to follow: on the succeeding lap Jeff took a sharp right-handed turn at the bottom of the main straight of the race, sending me head-first into a crowd of spectators. Jeff, single-minded as ever, didn't notice at first, but kindly stopped to pick me up on the next lap. All part of the rough and tumble of such a sport, if not a business. Given that sort of experience, however, it is little wonder that we were so able to pull together as a team in the later *Crayford* years.

*David McMullan in a race in 2010*

The Lambretta experience was a crucial forging point of our friendship and individual talents. The in-depth knowledge of certain key members of the staff at their Croydon works was as invaluable as it was impressive. Jock West was among the key engineers there. He'd been a director, as well as works rider, at A. J. S./Matchless, or AMC as it was known and had taken the Porcupine machine into second place in the Isle of Man senior race. His skill as a rider was still evident and he could maintain a stunning pace. After attempting to keep up with him down the lanes of Surrey during a Lambretta test, one visibly shaken rider told me: 'Don't ever try to follow that man!' Yet, during my long lunch chats with 'that man' it became clear to me just how entrenched and inflexible some of the older British motorcyclists were in their beliefs and attitudes. Jock was convinced that he knew exactly what the public wanted and, in his time, I am sure he was right. We had good-natured arguments on many points of technical detail. It was a time when an across-frame, multi-cylinder, electric start-bike was unthinkable as a production concept. When discussing the kart-racing chassis, he'd respond with a dictum bearing an endearing contradiction: 'Mac, to gain performance you have to add more lightness.' However, his emphatic instruction reflected a basic technical truth and it was always in the forefront of my mind when preparing for the international professional kart racing competitions. The pressing aim, then, was how to find ways of shaving off those extra pounds of chassis weight.

Our motorcycling interests played an important part in influencing the development of new *Crayford* projects. The Di Blasi, for instance, was an ingeniously designed motor scooter produced by a small Sicilian company, which was purpose-built to fold up neatly and be stored in a small space. We decided to import some of this model, renaming it the 'Crayford Puma Packaway' and designing our own cat-like puma badge to brand it.

*Puma folding motocycles prepared for sale*

Inevitably, this kind of project development involved a degree of trial and error before we got it right. In fact, it was one particular incident involving the machine which led directly to the introduction of an essential improvement. Eric Parker, a Yorkshireman and a biker who looked after our villa at Javea in Spain during the winter months, took out his host's Puma for a spin whilst staying at Jeff's Kent home at Old Hill House. Riding along the notoriously rough unsurfaced Chestnut Avenue at Tatsfield, the Puma's collapsible handlebars accidentally folded up, sending him flying. He bit the dust in the painful sense and ended up with a battered face. We, however, immediately put in place a specially designed *Crayford* steering lock in the front of the machine. This was fitted to all imported models from that moment onwards. Yet again, from a near-disaster emerged a design bonus. Twenty years later, the Di Blasis machines are still on sale in Spain, mainly in yacht clubs, specifically for carrying on board. I now note with some satisfaction that they are all equipped with a steering lock almost identical to the type we designed in Westerham, following Eric's bruising experience on that bumpy Kent lane all those years ago.

The Pumas sold fairly well, many of them to yacht owners because of their convenient packability. I myself always carried one, in its own *Crayford*-designed holdall bag, on my own Hirondelle catamaran. It was to prove a godsend during an alarming night-time Channel incident, just off the French coast. Gale-force winds had ripped both rudders off the cat, but I still managed to steer through the narrow harbour entrance at Gravelines on the French–Belgian border. My catamaran had been drifting sideways for two hours along the coast as gathering crowds of onlookers witnessed my plight, yet totally ignored my emergency distress flares. Finally, I managed to limp into the harbour and drop anchor. I then secured the vessel and headed off to Calais by road on my handy *Crayford* Packaway Puma. Looks of bemused amazement greeted me, as I queued for the ferry, still uncomfortably attired in full sailing waterproofs and with my trusty midget scooter at my side.

*The BMC 1800/2200 hatchback conversion enjoyed a 12-year production run*

# Chapter 15

# 'Shifty' Sales

Our inimitable Spanish distributor, Francis Alcaraz, typically came up with a product which was to prove quite a weighty challenge. Known as the 'Shifty', this motorcycle was equipped with a huge and powerful Fiat engine. Jeff immediately became involved, travelling to Italy to organise a sole UK concession deal on the machine and then bringing the bike back with him. It was quite monstrously powerful, yet a rewarding and smooth riding experience.

In view of its size and weight, the Shifty was declared out of bounds to our staff at the Westerham works. Typically, there was one apprentice who could not resist the temptation to give it a quick burst around the factory yard. Not for long though: he dropped it, no doubt defeated and in awe of its raw power and size. Jeff returned to find it lying heavily on its side. Instinctively, he gripped hold of one end of the handlebar to pull the machine upright. Now Jeff was a strong man, but even with his muscle power he was only able to bend the handlebar into a vertical position. It took a major team effort to move the giant Shifty back on to its wheels. In a sense, that clearly demonstrated the machine's fundamental weakness. Its engine part and general technical similarities to the Fiat would have been good selling points, but this beast was just too heavy and consequently not a good handler.

The most profitable *Crayford* motorcycle venture was unquestionably the huge Yamaha VMAX. I had spotted one displayed in a large motorcycle showroom near Toronto Airport, through which I passed on one of my visits to ODG in Ontario – an enormously powerful machine and a non-imported model of a type I had not previously seen in Europe. I purchased it there and then as it had barely been used and was in near-perfect condition. It then sat in our Westerham works in Kent, whilst I went on holiday. In response to an enquiry about this impressive, if unused monster, I agreed to sell. I asked – and got – about £1500 more than it had cost us and promptly ordered another from the same Toronto showroom. That one, too, sold quickly and it wasn't long before a steady stream of profitable VMAX sales followed.

We were the sole sales source for the machine in Britain. Oddly, though, despite its huge attraction and qualities, I never owned a VMAX myself and never even rode one on the open road. We did, however, sell the machine on unusual terms. Each customer was asked to sign a document stating that the purchase was without warranty back-up. More than that, they were also required to accept that no spare parts or after-sales service would be available in the UK. It was quite extraordinary that our clients should accept these conditions, but they did.

For some reason, after selling *Crayford* and my subsequent retirement from the business in 1987, the new owners dropped this highly profitable line, concluding – correctly perhaps – that their time would be better spent concentrating on the successful Argocat and increasing its sales. This they achieved. The new owners weren't 'bikers' and motorcycles held little interest for them. No more VMAX machines came into Britain for a long time after that.

Motorcycles somehow brought out both the best and the worst in Jeff. One unforgettable incident occurred when we were travelling to Africa for the 3,000 mile Trans-Sahara Southern Cross Rally. We were accompanied by my sons, Peter and Sean on BMWs, as well as Jeff's son, Rick – in his sidecar.

Already annoyed by red tape and the attitude of French customs at Calais, the inevitable clash was brewing when one officer angrily beckoned him to return to the far end of the customs shed, where his colleagues were standing in a group. Jeff yelled at me: 'Get on' and I crouched down beside him in the open-framed competition sidecar he had specially built for the Sahara event. He then fired up the BMW and roared off down the length of the customs hall at full power. Only some 50 ft. from the assembled officers did he then apply full lock and we ploughed on with a screaming front tyre, halting a few feet from the group. I was terrified by this dangerous display, as were the customs officers. I was also furious with 'Jeffery' as I called him when angry with him. Having spent months getting our three solo machines plus side cars ready for the North African rally, here he was quite needlessly putting the whole trip in jeopardy before we had even left the French Channel port.

Further spectaculars followed on reaching Marseilles. Returning from a coffee break to the large station car park, I found my no. 2 son, Sean, giving a crowd of French onlookers a virtuoso, impromptu display of 'wheelies' with his heavily laden BMW, riding the powerful machine in roaring fashion on its back tyre. I took this philosophically, as I did other outbursts of passion and emotion, in the belief that both in business and family relations you cannot simply select the 'good bits' from an individual. You have to accept and work with the 'whole character package', qualities, weaknesses and all.

This judgement applied as much to the tirelessly inventive, if ever restless, Jeff, as it did to Sean. Their drive and initiative formed an integral part of their distinctive personalities. If, as then, the 18-year-old and irrepressible Sean was prepared to tackle the desert on a superbike, then perhaps it also follows that the same highly-charged person will also on occasion need to let off steam.

Whether on or off a motorcycle, Sean was a real 'go-getter' and it perhaps follows that he was not an easy youngster to live with when growing up. At just seven years of age he issued his first ultimatum on some now long forgotten issue – and left home. The sandwiches carefully prepared by my wife, Maureen, for his 'running away' journey only lasted as far as the village green in Tatsfield. By the time he had reached the bus stop, he was both bored and hungry and returned home for fresh supplies. He then became involved in some other distraction in the garage and the threatened junior trek to foreign parts was quickly abandoned and forgotten.

Jeff's children, Rick and Cath, were never that keen on the 'biker' business, but in our case, though, it was in the family blood. Peter, my eldest, shares this passion, albeit in a way which reflects his own personality: steady, cautious and someone who has developed over the years into a first-class rider and driver. Yet it was my daughter, Sarah, who came up with the biggest surprise of all. As a child, she simply used to sit, thumb in mouth, quietly watching the boys as they zoomed around the house on their mini-motorcycles, but how things can change! Today, the woman who never had shown any interest in machines now rides a powerful Triumph. Sarah probably possesses more accomplished road-craft skills than any of us from experience gained as a police officer in South London. During her training she turned out to be a highly skilled driver and came out top on her advanced Met driving course at Hendon Police College. The motorcycling tradition which had played such a significant part in the history of *Crayford* continues through the family.

With more than fifty years of road and competition experience behind me, my own passion for motorcycles remains undiminished, although a progressively deteriorating eye condition is now threatening to curb my 'biking' activities. It was a source of great joy and satisfaction for me, though, when in 2004 both my sons, Peter and Sean, came over from California to Spain to join me in a magnificent motorcycling tour in the mountains west of the Costa Blanca.

*A Ford Fiesta Fly*

# Chapter 16

# Ones that got away

Innovative ideas were always at the forefront of our planning at *Crayford* . It was inevitable, however, that quite a few of these ideas and plans never made it beyond the drawing board. This approach demonstrates just how persistant we were in our search for new avenues, using and developing our own technical improvements. Did I say drawing board? Well, it could take some unlikely forms, sometimes a damp beer mat at The Ship in Tatsfield, or a paper tablecloth in the Caracole Restaurant, just off the Ramblas in Barcelona. More often than not, Jeff would be with me at such times when the ideas flowed almost as readily as the beer.

'Stretching' the two-door Porsche 911 to a four-door version was one such idea which initially seemed so attractive, and yet the original drawing lay around for quite some time. Perhaps the project could have worked as initially conceived, given that it emerged before the introduction of highly sophisticated electronics. The fact was that its rear-mounted engine design would have meant that we could have successfully 'cut and shut' a wiring loom for a radical 'stretching' form of mechanical surgery. One somewhat unexpected problem though: I never liked the Porsche. Nonetheless, we did have some at *Crayford.* I found the models of that time had terrifyingly unreliable brakes when cold and that the handling was unforgiving in the extreme. No doubt these weaknesses are now things of the past and have long since been rectified. In any event, the four-door was my first idea, quickly followed by a plan for a stretch model. I considered it ideal for the American market (where stretching is big business), though Ferry Porsche (builder of the first sports car by the famed German maker) would surely have turned in his grave at such a prospect.

Stretching, however, was not something we got involved in. It lacked appeal for me, although today the concept is becoming more acceptable in the UK. Nonetheless, I had a good relationship with Colman Milnes, the firm involved in stretching work on Fords and the thought did strike me in those early days that it may have been a mistake to focus on convertibles instead of stretch vehicles and station wagons.

Yet another potentially lucrative idea we failed to follow up was the Mercedes pick-up. Built to a high standard and equipped with the right 'platform', it could have been a very acceptable vehicle for, say, a wealthy farmer in Australia or perhaps the Beverley Hills golfer who is keen to turn up at the club behind the wheel of something different and suitably up-market.

Such a project would have turned on the old percentage game, i.e. just 1% of the market would guarantee a profitable return. We had the necessary technology in our Westerham factory, but somehow never got round to it. However, it is something which I have mentioned as a project to my sons in America, so maybe they will follow up the idea at some point.

Another pick-up idea focused on the Jaguar XJS, the aim being to construct a low, long camping trailer at the rear – 'American-style' in design – with a large pivot in the back of the pick-up, to enable the trailer to be unhitched. Such an arrangement would have given the vehicle a dual function: practical purposes by day, yet easy for the evening drive into town. The pivot for the trailer assembly in the middle of the pick-up platform is a design which the Americans exploit and market with notable success. The end result would have been a smart, high performance 'rig' if equipped with the right type of suspension, boasting the merit of functioning as a 'good handler' at speed. All in all, a promising idea, but which never materialised and I am not sure I even got as far as producing an initial drawing.

Unlikely as it may sound, the amphibious Ford Fiesta was one project which we did develop at *Crayford,* although I doubt whether we had any deep or serious intention of actually putting it into production, perhaps with good reason. A photograph of Jeff trying to climb out of the one of the vehicles we built, as it sank beneath the waves, still survives in our archives.

Then there was the 'Short Fiesta'. The idea here was to take perhaps eighteen inches out of the centre of the vehicle, virtually eliminate the back seat capacity altogether and give it a great turn-in-a-circle capability. Time has proven that this was a highly feasible idea, as demonstrated by today's vehicles such as the Smart car, a motor with virtually no space in the back, yet slim enough to park almost anywhere and capable of turning in the tightest of road spaces.

My idea for the 'add-on starting handle' was based on the

experience in many countries, where something as simple as a flat battery can pose insuperable problems, as the battery cannot be changed or the engine just fails to start for whatever reason. The absence of the old trusty starting handle seemed to me a crazy omission, especially so with small 1 or 1.2 litre engines, which in an emergency can easily be turned over and fired into action. By then I had already started devising a starting handle kit for the export Fiesta model, or whatever Ford was selling successfully in the more remote overseas markets.

Starting problems had occurred in our Snow Goose catamaran, most notably when Jeff and a few friends headed across to Holland one night, leaving me at home lying on my back in bed temporarily immobilised with laminectomy problems. Having reached the entrance to Flushing harbour in Holland, they discovered that they had exhausted the batteries and were unable to start the vessel, despite being powered by a standard diesel engine. This experience suggested a simple technical loophole which sorely needed to be filled. Happily, I had developed a marine ply and Fafnir bearings kit to enable the diesel engine to be started and this device could be assembled over an engine bay in less than 5 minutes, offering an easy start procedure if a propane gas heater was suspended in the engine air intake.

I had other ideas as well for fast-starting the Snow Goose, one being to haul a plastic container of water up the mast on a winch and then drop it, employing the fast rotation of the halliard to spin over the engine. Oddly enough, I came across a similar idea in use in Africa many years later. In this case, the local Africans continued to use a diesel engine long after its original battery had disappeared, by bolting in position a tyre-less car wheel, wrapped around with rope. Some 30 or 40 Africans would then charge down the hill – where the engine was located – pulling the rope round the wheel rim and firing the engine into life. Sadly, I didn't have time to stay and watch this battery-less firing method in action for any length of time, but I would have loved to discover what happened when the engine fired and the rope continued to wrap itself round the wheel. Presumably some unfortunate Africans would have been swiftly dragged back up the hill again.

In the 1960s, when we both had young families, Jeff and I grew tired of the way the children's push trucks and toboggans were so quickly wrecked. So, we designed a four-wheel truck which could be steered down a hill by foot controls. And then, when turned upside down and the wheels removed, the trucks were immediately converted into a superb toboggan. Plastic coated to a high standard, they were made to last and strong enough to bear almost any weight. For years afterwards the trucks were used to move furniture around the house and garden. This was yet another potentially successful *Crayford* idea which never made it into the market place.

One key idea, however, which did get out there (albeit in the hands of other manufacturers) was the child's car seat – the first one to be placed on the passenger seat in a way which enabled the youngster to use the adult safety belts correctly. For use in either the front or back seat, it was developed at the *Crayford* works. Just one or two were custom-made of foam and trimmed with leather cloth to match the interior of the vehicle. I put one to extensive use myself as a car seat for my eldest son, Peter, in the 1960s, well ahead of later mass-market models.

The Mark II child's car seat model we developed was especially successful and – as far as I am aware – the first of its kind in Europe. Instead of mounting it on the passenger seat, we designed a special steel frame which fitted just behind the shoulder of the driver and front seat passenger, in the rear of the car. In this case, the 'tunnel' safety mounting points were used as the lower mounting fixtures, which offered the positive advantage of the child being easily reached by the front seat passenger. The metal work reached back to the rear parcel shelf. We personally found this arrangement worked admirably when the children were young 'sparring' partners, as it effectively separated Sean and Peter and brought their punching exchanges to a halt – at least in the car!

The instant left-hand drive conversion we designed was yet another promising idea aimed at solving a problem unique to the British on Continental driving holidays: arriving in France and having to adapt immediately to re-defined driving conditions, with the steering wheel on the 'wrong' side. We started by bringing in Belgian-made Ford Fiestas and converting them from left to right-hand drive for use on English roads. This steering wheel switch-over was not a difficult engineering operation and for some time it did earn us some money.

The technical thinking behind this was the idea that we could take a standard popular-make car, such as one in the Ford range, and introduce a conversion kit which enabled the owner, en-route for Dover, to call in to *Crayford* where, within a couple of hours, his vehicle could be converted to a left-hand drive. Logistically, this was not a major problem with our factory conveniently based in the middle of Kent. The instant change-over concept would allow the driver to enjoy a holiday in France without having to worry about all the obvious personal safety factors and attendant insurance problems. Indeed, it could even eliminate the need for the premium excesses eagerly imposed by the insurance companies.

However, there was one aspect which I had not completely thought through, that being the need to specify that our conversion was available on automatic transmission models only and these were not a popular choice at the time. Nevertheless, it was undoubtedly an original idea, and I believe there would have been demand for converting cars of that era. In my mind's eye it would have all worked out so neatly: on the return journey the customer could call in at our works in Kent and we would make the change back over to right-hand drive. In addition, the special parts needed for the conversion would be kept for his next continental tour or we would buy them back from him.

The bench seat removal facility was yet another idea which, for some reason or another, slipped through our fingers. The BMC 1800 hatchback series, which we had been building successfully for some 12 years, incorporated an especially novel feature and one which no-one had thought of imitating for some time. This was a one-piece lift out rear seat assembly. All it needed was a reasonably strong man or two individuals to easily lift the bench seat from the back of the 1800 – in a mere ten seconds – and immediately have the benefit of a greater space. This versatile vehicle, or Land Crab as we called it, had enormous rear capacity with a low floor which was widely appreciated by our customers. At that time, this feature was quite unique and not copied by any of our competitors until much later.

Looking back now, I can see how good we were at introducing novel ideas into the British market and on one occasion we were actually helped with Government money. We developed the concept of integral rear side windows on the Audi convertibles, meaning that the rear quarter 'lights' or side windows were permanent fixtures on the convertible hood mechanism. However, when the hood was down these windows disappeared with the mechanism. This disadvantage was offset by the benefit arising from the elimination of the shaking or vibration problems. The fact that this enabled the hood fabric or canopy to be fixed semi-permanently to the rear quarter lights was an additional bonus.

Yet another promising idea, but one that never went into production, was the 'Girlie' button, a term which doubtless would now produce frowns of disapproval from the feminist or politically correct lobby. This project was, in fact, very much in my mind during the final years before selling *Crayford* in the mid-1980s. I had long noticed that women drivers had difficulty coping with the heavy steering of models with oversized tyres.

In particular I was thinking of those on the high performance Fiesta models. As a tyre wears, the 'scrub' area or amount of rubber on the road surface, increases, making low-speed parking manoeuvres exceedingly difficult. To overcome this, I planned to introduce an instant pump which would operate for perhaps 15–20 seconds, producing the power steering facility whenever the speedometer was reading less than 10 mph. For the same reason drivers in vehicles such as the VW Golf GTI would have found this accessory of benefit.

Eventually, however, power steering became standard on many cars, so this would probably have put paid to the conversion kit idea anyway. Although, interestingly, in more recent years one major manufacturer has indeed introduced such an adaptation to solve this very steering problem. From the manufacturer's viewpoint, power steering installation is on a par with air-conditioning if the factory is properly 'tooled up' to install the 'extra'. The percentage of vehicles fitted with this accessory continues to increase and so then it becomes a practical proposition to supply it as a standard accessory, the cost increase having become almost negligible.

Mooring hooks also occupied my thoughts, even though they had nothing to do with cars. I can still clearly recall that this idea occurred to me as I was falling asleep one night on the Snow Goose catamaran off Harty Ferry in Kent. It was surely time, I was thinking sleepily, that yachtsmen should be able to loop a rope through a ring on top of a mooring buoy at, say six feet distance, haul it back and secure the line on board, thus ensuring that this 'running line' was then available when casting off the following morning.With the idea still in my head, I returned to the works at Westerham on Monday and, as I was inclined to do, grabbed Tony, my Development Engineer. Dragging him away to his work bench, he could then apply his inventive mind to this, my latest project. Tony was brilliant at working on impromptu ideas and we developed a superb gadget designed to enable a yachtsman to pass a rope around another rope (which may itself be some 6–8 feet away) and then bring it back on board, feeding through the steel ring on top of the mooring buoy. On this occasion, though, other more pressing business matters subsequently intervened and the project was temporarily shelved. Yet, somewhat frustratingly, the self-same sort of device appeared on the market within a year. I was filled with a deep sense of dismay, having earlier taken the precaution of investigating the issue through our patent agent and established – as far as one could – that nothing like it already existed, or at least had not been registered at the time. However, I was aware that the Snow Goose experience was clearly taking us in other new and exciting directions and there were a number of good ideas, which we did try over the years, which might have made money.

Of all the 'ones that got away', it was the Mercedes pick-up truck which I would like to have seen make the grade. Had we taken the production level to its huge potential and secured the all-important Mercedes warranty (achievable through the reputation of our estate car business), there would have undoubtedly been a steady market, especially in South America, the United States, Australia and maybe other territories as well. Undoubtedly, though, the existence of stringent tests and conditions affecting type approval would have presented us with some formidable hurdles to overcome as we developed the product.

And yet even nowadays, with all the curbs and limitations imposed by regulations, I am convinced that if I were to produce a good-looking Mercedes pickup to Daimler Benz quality standards, it would sell. I make these observations in the light of the growing number of comments in both the motoring press and public surveys of recent years, all of which question the quality level of the latest generation of Mercedes cars and the 'A' class model. There are genuine causes for complaint among Mercedes range customers. So, I have to say that if we were still in business on the level which I enjoyed, I definitely would be inclined to pay more attention to the products of the Japanese car giant, Toyota. For my personal use I would prefer to carry on with Mercedes. I believe I am on my tenth.

Clearly, such a judgement is a subjective one, tempered here by a lifetime's business experience at the sharp end of an always difficult global business. Still, I have to admit to certain deep and unhappy feelings when I myself am obliged to support the Japanese industry, whether occasionally riding, as I do, Japanese motorcycles and – sometimes – even owning a Japanese car.

No doubt many of my generation suffer from the same feeling of unease – even 60 years on – when supporting businessmen whose forebears had, without hesitation, tortured Allied prisoners during the Second World War. Nevertheless, forgiveness is something one has to learn, certainly so in the field of global business, where pragmatism is dictated by the demands of market forces.

Within that context I would indeed be inclined to look very closely at the increasingly impressive Toyota range to find a commercial opportunity for an estate car pickup or convertible. The Japanese – and even more so the Chinese – constitute the emerging threat to the entire European and American motor industry. Undeniably, the quality of the Toyota product range is quite awesome. The dramatic collapse of MG Rover at Longbridge in April 2005, bears out some of those broader fears concerning the huge challenge to the industry from the Far East.

Most of the 'ones that got away' in this chapter, I would have been happy to see go through R and D, to short run and finally full production stages.

There is one exception however: the Ferrari project. In the early 1970s Ferrari had brought into Britain a number of their high performance cars in convertible form. We were contacted as convertible specialists and told in great confidence that the new cars had been parked in the open and there was 'serious water ingress', in other words, they leaked like sieves.

Jeff and I were invited over to the head office, south of London, for an urgent meeting and taken out to a pleasant lunch. The Ferrari directors decided it would be a good idea if Jeff and I each drove one of the new cars; so we did. When we arrived at the smart hotel for lunch both Jeff and I said we needed to use the toilet. I will never forget the following few minutes. Jeff was standing relieving himself some distance from me. After a few seconds he turned and looked at me with that steady gaze of disbelief which I knew so well and nodded his head from side to side. He didn't say a word; he didn't need to. His look said 'run a mile', in other words: 'this stuff is awful.'

They kindly gave us a car to take back to Westerham for evaluation to see what we could do about the rain leak problems. We had no chance to talk on the way back as we were in separate cars. When we got to the factory we walked round the Ferrari in silence, as far as I can remember. The real quality giveaway was that one side of the car was different from the other. This is the sort of examination that the public never carries out. In this case, for example, the window on the driver's door was at a very different height to that on the passenger side with the inevitable roof sealing problem. And so on. The panel gapping was very hit-and-miss and we both found the car hard to drive with poor pedal location and rough gear selection. As Jeff said: ' an impressive car outside the pub, but you couldn't actually use it to go anywhere.' There was no sensible luggage space and the interior was rather cramped. In those days before the manufacturer had learned from Mr. Chapman to make suspension that would keep the wheels on the road with low unsprung weight ratio and a soft ride, the only way was a stiff suspension setup and and a fairly harsh ride. This Ferrari, of course, had just that.

Nowadays things have changed dramatically and I still find it hard to believe just how well a comfortable family car such as the Focus or Golf handle and how clean and gentle the feedback, when either the front or rear tyre slip angles are reached. Both these cars can be induced to adopt under- or oversteer smoothly and with control, even in the hands of an amateur like myself. The Focus is quite astonishing.

Since that early Ferrari experience there has been a giant leap forward in build quality, ride and handling. The NVH (noise, vibration and harshness) levels of thirty years ago are no longer acceptable in modern vehicle engineering. N and V are objective criteria and can be measured fairly easily. Harshness, however, is subjective and uses 'clinics' to provide subjective human impressions. This second area of investigation is known as psychoacoustics. So it is no wonder that modern Mondeo Man really has it made.

We decided against getting involved with Ferrari and returned the car with our apologies.

A final idea that would have been totally revolutionary and which is still with me to this day, is the concept of a convertible roof for a car that is held in place by air pressure rather than by a steel frame. The normal steel links of the mechanism would be replaced by narrow inflated tubes. Modern family saloons that can travel at over 100 mph with ease obviously present something of a challenge when made into a convertible, because of laminar flow effect and the hood frame and window sealing would have to be of a high standard.

But there is room for investigation here. If people can fling themselves off a boat into the ocean in an emergency, relying on a life jacket with air pressure and electronically welded seams, then this reliability does exist. The idea came to me from sitting for long hours in the cockpit of yachts, looking at my life jacket which used this very system. If I am sent back into this world, I might have a go at the world's first pneumatic hood frame!

# Chapter 17

# Managing Crayford

One tale about Henry Ford sums up the inherent difficulties of this business. It is said that he became so frustrated at the inability of his vast accounts department to give him a short-term verdict about how well or badly the company was performing that, one morning, his accounts staff arrived at work to find their office closed and all their furniture and filing cabinets dumped in a heap in the car park. It was a legendary way of making a point, one which has indeed a universal application.

From the majors to the minors. In our own small way, Jeff and I came to at least a related conclusion: most companies seem to go bust either through miscalculation on the part of their advertising consultants or their accountants. It is extraordinary just how many companies collapse, even when they are producing a good product. A study of the Mercedes car history offers a clear pointer. The company continued to make millions of profit, only to find that this surplus was siphoned off into various non-car ventures, precipitating a globally successful company into near bankruptcy.

Our own approach at *Crayford* was always to keep a close watch on the financial map. From our earliest days, I produced a monthly financial analysis designed to show how much the business – stock and work in progress – was really worth, if it had to be sold almost instantaneously, even in the middle of a project. Projects can collapse at an advanced stage or in mid-production.

In recent years, readers will be aware of the film *The Perfect Storm*, based on the disaster that overcame a fishing trawler and illustrating the catastrophic results of being hit from three different directions simultaneously – something which I know about only too well myself and which is very relevant to the business world.

There are various potential disaster scenarios, almost too numerous to detail. A couple might suffice though here. One example is when a project is almost finished and then, out of the blue, your trading currency hardens in a manner which quite literally can stop your exports overnight.

Another example: without any advance warning the Australian government decides to change the law on rear safety belt mounting points, just when all the 'tooling' for all your Australia-bound order has been completed on the rear quarter panels. In these circumstances you might only have a few days to solve the resulting problems before shipment.

In the world of sailing, the 'triple crisis' is a well-known phenomenon. If one thing goes wrong, beware. If two go awry, then a third is almost inevitable. During the many thousands of miles Maureen and I sailed our Snow Goose catamaran, we encountered this same unnerving trio of circumstances a number of times.

On one occasion we had sailed down the North Sea from the Scheldt Estuary and were about to enter the Thames. It was 03.00h when, amid high seas and strong winds, part of the rigging snapped. Time for Plan B to be put into action – that is, to start up the Volvo engine. Not an option I favoured, because of long personal experience of its unreliability. My fears were soon borne out. Within a few minutes it had 'dropped a valve', for which it was noted. We were floundering in heavy seas, with no sail power, no engine and where it was too dangerous and deep to drop anchor.

In times of crisis, Maureen usually would declare with an air of homely reassurance: 'What about a cup of tea?' This was no exception and down she went into the galley to boil the kettle. Within a minute we had run out of gas. We were in the 'triple crisis'. But Lady Luck was on our side and, despite all, we battled on and managed to limp home through the entrance to Ramsgate Harbour under headsail. The maxim that 'things happen in threes' has a wide application.

A key factor in management, as I saw it, was staff motivation and administration. I always tried to have a personal, uninterrupted talk with each member of our *Crayford* team, at least once every six months, the aim being to find what he or she felt needed improving or whether a personal problem needed addressing. My wife's experience as a doctor was hugely instructive. She used to say that patients are surprisingly reluctant to tell a doctor about the true nature of their problem, giving rise to the phenomenon which she called the 'door handle' stage of consultation. As the patient is leaving, with a hand on the door handle, they would often turn round and add, ' Yes, there's one small thing'. More often than not, that 'small thing' was in fact the real reason for the appointment, often something deeply personal or a source of embarrassment.

It was not unusual to find the same reaction occurring when I sat down with a member of staff for a chat. Sometimes you had to dig deep to get to the heart of the problem. Unsurprisingly, though, most problems related to the subject of wages, a point confirmed by other employers. Job satisfaction was secondary: it was the money, above all, which counted. Nevertheless, these chats with staff members often revealed other problems of a personal nature, not directly connected with the business at all.

The chat strategy worked in other ways, notably when

someone was patently unhappy about an issue on the workshop floor. In this case, I would offer to bring forward the next scheduled staff meeting or simply ask if we could wait until there was time for a more in-depth conversation about the problem. I always felt it was important to show genuine concern on my part as well as offer reassurance that the issue troubling the individual would not get swept under the carpet.

Keeping the size of our operation relatively small was part of an instinctive survival policy. We preferred to remain at a level where the factory was bursting at the seams rather than embark on an expansion programme. A staff level of some 30 employees was our upper limit, a unit which enabled Jeff and me, together with the foreman, to most comfortably cope with whatever problems arose. There was an even more pressing external reason for this caution. At the time we were also witnessing the major source of our livelihoods, the ever-troubled British motor industry, almost collapsing around our ears. To us it seemed very clear that much of it stemmed from a deeply insular approach, as if the designers of many British cars had never left England, the land of smooth roads and temperate climate. It was rumoured that one of Britain's leading and most famous car designers had only been to London twice in his life and had no intention of travelling that far again. He was at that time designing a well-known British family car that had no provision for a radio. Enough said.

In locations such as Nairobi or Mombasa, where the French-built Peugeot taxis could thunder up and down almost impassable roads for years, the Morris 1100, for example, would be rendered useless within a week. Our visits to Canada were always enlivened by talks of someone trying to run a new Jaguar. The Americans used to say: 'Always buy two, one to use while the other one is getting fixed.' Sadly, even after all these years, matters do not appear to have improved that much. Only recently, my sons needed a new body panel for a current Jaguar model they were repairing in Los Angeles. No such part was available in the States and the client was advised he would have to wait until one could be brought in with the next shipment from the UK. It is hard to believe that such shortcomings still exist, but they do.

Yet there are contradictions here. The engineering expertise, for example, which lay behind the remarkable RAF success in the Battle of Britain, based on the unbeatable Rolls Royce engines of the Spitfire and Hurricane planes – as well as, without a doubt, the outstanding bravery of the young men who flew them. Then there is the little-known fact that it was the British-built Merlin engine, introduced into the US Mustang Fighter, which gave the US Air Force the extra range with drop tanks and power to dominate the skies over Berlin in the crucial later stages of the Second World War.

That sort of engineering expertise is still there. Even now, the majority of the high-performance engines for the Indianapolis race in the US are still built by small companies in the south east of England. We at *Crayford* were of that breed. We stayed small and it worked. Remaining a compact unit helped us to survive the difficult times which afflicted the British motor industry. In contrast to these huge factories, we could be flexible, change direction quickly and grab any opportunity which might appear. Growth of the business was always on our minds, though, and quite often Jeff and I would look at our customer waiting lists and discuss the possibility of expanding the factory. However, we avoided the temptation and kept the place bursting at the seams instead. To me it seemed that a natural management hurdle arises when handling a unit of more than 30. Unquestionably, there are distinct advantages which flow from handling compact and highly flexible and adaptable formations – of 30 to 40 men, something which perhaps the military discovered a long time ago, going right back to the times of the Roman army and continuing up to the modern-day British Army, with its platoons and companies of men.

With a small team, you can read the warning signs early on and appreciate just how individuals, when in trouble, adopt different ways of putting across points or concerns. A welder, for example, might start complaining bitterly about the 'flux coating' on his welding rods, when in reality the problem is more to do with meeting his car insurance bill. And where female employees are concerned – we employed several in the accounts and secretarial areas, as well as in the Trim Shop – the deeper truth was not always easy to uncover. Speaking from a male point of view, I found their reactions more complex. Yet, as a result of our own brand of personal management, there was also a deep and fierce loyalty factor at work, most notably in the person of our secretary, Sally, one of those who would be prepared to 'fight tooth and nail' to protect the business and all it involved. It could be almost described as a fanatical sense of loyalty, a difficult concept for many men to comprehend – the instinct to protect, be it the boss at work or the children at home. What I did learn about women employees, however, was that any problems were best resolved immediately, on the spot, whereas male workers would be content with a promise to explore the issue in detail at the next meeting.

Punctuality was always a key issue in the smooth running of our operation. I sought to introduce the concept that 'on time is too late', based on the management philosophy that completing a job just on time leaves no room for the 'what ifs'. Introducing such an approach was not always easy. Sometimes I found myself having to lie and bring a job completion date forward by 24 hours to ensure a car was actually ready on time. The obvious drawback to this approach, of course, was that 'crying wolf' too often gives out a signal to everyone that you are prepared to be economical with the truth – never a good management tactic.

Another management approach I tried to introduce at *Crayford* was to foresee problems and prevent them arising in the first place, rather than having to deal with them later in a crisis situation. As already described earlier, diversification played an important part in our management strategy, even more so in view of the unease we felt about our dependence on the British Motor Industry as it stumbled from one crisis to another. Its core problem was one of quality and the new Triumph Stag I had bought for Maureen was a prime example of the difficulties one encountered with British cars. Within a week of purchase it had developed electrical problems. I can clearly recall sitting in the front seat with Jeff, as we lifted the electrics out of the centre console, only to discover that some of the wires had been joined by twisting and wrapping them together with ordinary PVC tape – not even self-amalgamating tape. This was quite beyond belief and Jeff said so in the strongest language.

We just had to look elsewhere. The diversification trail took me on many travels and visits to foreign exhibitions, where I stumbled across a number of money-spinning products that could be imported or ideas which could be adapted and improved upon. Thus we came to be involved in the LGP (low ground pressure) ATV (all terrain vehicle) business and the highly successful Argocat vehicle. As it turned out, this was our most important 'diversion' project which effectively saved our company and ensured our subsequent success. Here it is worth noting that at that time, in the 1960s the Jeep, Land Rover and the farm tractor were the only ATVs available for use by the general public.

As already mentioned in an earlier chapter, and in complete contrast, the portable Pandero stove from Albacete in Spain was another of our unusual ventures. The product was bought in at £13 and sold well for a rather comfortable £65. And then there were the 'bread and butter' products, such as the Cortina and the hatchback BMC 1800, a conversion in production at our Westerham works for a long period and I believe I am correct in saying that it was the first large hatchback in Britain.

But it was the ATV market which proved to be key for us. The secret was the combination of lightweight manufacturing material, balloon tyres and, above all, a lightweight modern engine and transmission systems, which enabled the development of a vehicle capable of carrying several people, foodstuffs or other materials needed for transporting stranded animals or similar across bog land, soft snow or in steep mountainous conditions, where not even Land Rovers and Jeeps could travel. This was the world which Jeff and I knew well, having between us spent thousands of hours in off-road motorcycling. No better way can exist to learn the lessons of weight and traction than climbing rocky and muddy slope terrain in this manner. We were naturals for this type of vehicle. However, during the early years of the Argocat development, we were also acutely aware of how hugely important it was to maintain alongside our Argocat work the manufacture of our other bread-and-butter, constant-run products.

Work on developing the Argocat was not all plain sailing. Initially we were not that confident about its potential success, especially after the Amphicat referred to in a previous chapter, had been such a reliability disaster. In my career I had over the years often observed other entrepreneurs' attempt to launch new products and get businesses up and running, only to fail. Common sense had to prevail and, as in our case, an existing source of income from permanent employment helped us to survive. The kart-racing equipment and the Mini convertible were all products which I had started producing in my own time, whilst still employed by Lambretta Trojan and, looking back now to 1962, I can see that my approach then to a new business venture was quite a bold one.

Constant-run products were always our main production goal. As the months turned into years, the men in the works would settle down to a productive work pattern. The staff, it seemed to me, were at home and at ease carrying out the same work every week. Change and upheaval were not welcome, the latter often a recipe for matters going wrong. As a hands-on manager you soon become aware that a workman welding in chassis members or making the convertible will eventually find a quicker or more efficient way to do the job. And this is where the 'innovation bonus' would come as a welcome reward, as I slipped £10 notes into overall pockets with the comment 'good thinking…'.

There is also the exponential curve factor: put very simply, the longer you market something, the more people hear about it, thus increasing the number of potential buyers. Even with a good product, though, it can be a slow burner. Press coverage and word-of-mouth recommendation can take a long time – years perhaps – especially so in our case, for news of a new *Crayford* Mercedes to reach a dealership or private customer in Australia. Ultimately, we found that enquiries about a product would come in from all over the world. It just took time.

The constant-run pattern also left Jeff and me free to focus and develop new products, even if some bordered on the crazy, as in the case of our plan to convert small Ford Fiestas into amphibious vehicles. Yet projects such as this introduced a relaxed atmosphere into the factory for a few weeks and it became a popular joke among staff that the Fiesta prototype sank with Jeff inside. This spectacularly unsuccessful experiment was conducted more than 30 years ago, in secrecy, on Felbridge Lake, near East Grinstead. To my astonishment, only last year I was confronted by a friend in Spain, who told me how many years ago he had witnessed a curious scene whilst walking his dog near a lake in England – a group of men pushing a Ford Fiesta into the water! So we did have an uninvited spectator at the scene after all! I had to confess and tell him the truth. This supported the theory I have always held, in business and in personal affairs: 'In the end, everybody knows everything'. It is a useful principle. One that perhaps our banking and finance industries might adopt!

Maintaining good morale among the staff was always on

our mind. We developed this consciously by the 'play together stay together' principle, which we encouraged with works outings to France and the 'in-house' Christmas Party, which sometimes got rather out of hand. At one of the latter one woman guest went missing. A search party was despatched to scour the darkened factory, only to find her in the back of a rocking, partly-built Mercedes estate. I fear it was actually her husband who discovered her. On another occasion, as the party finished, a lady member of staff needed a lift home. Jeffrey's Rover was the only convenient car, so off she and I went. She was going to be sick, she said, so I told her to do it out of the window. But it all went wrong. She couldn't get the window down without releasing the safety belt to reach forward to wind it down and she vomited all over the belt as it retracted into its holder.The next morning a member of the workshop staff had the unenviable job of cleaning up a terrible mess; not helped by the fact that the Rover carpet could not be removed for cleaning without major interior dismantling.

The 'play together stay together' technique did pay off, as we managed to hold our staff for long periods. A ten-year employment run was quite common at *Crayford* . I believe also that this loyalty was fostered by our own participation on the factory floor – Jeff's in particular. He was following what I regard as rule number one in business: 'be there'. He would spend an entire day working with one or two of the men on whatever new project was in hand, or making a new jig to speed up the installation process on one of our convertibles. In fact, it was not easy to get him to sit down in the office and go through the paperwork or budget figures. He was happiest when in overalls, enjoying a tea break in the canteen with the men, his welding goggles perched on top of his thinning hair and his powerful arms grimy with oil. On such occasions he would invariably be discussing the merits of various beers. He used to say: 'There's no such thing as bad beer – it's just that some beer is better than others.' I firmly believe that this sort of daily involvement with the men on the workshop floor helped prevent us from suffering the traditional 'them and us' attitude, which so bedevilled workplace relationships in British industry at that time. It was also part of my personal philosophy that 'you can't just pick the good bits out of people.' When we employed someone we took on the whole package with his or her personal problems and personality quirks.

But the British 'Two Nations' social divide still seems ingrained and it is said that in Britain today the poor are increasing in numbers and the really wealthy are increasingly wealthy. Not a formula for a peaceful future. I first came across this damaging approach after just 12 weeks' basic training as a National Serviceman in the RAF in 1956, when I found myself with the rank of Pilot Officer. It was not a comfortable feeling – a distinct 'them and us' resentment that seemed to be fostered among the other ranks towards those of us who had been to public school or university, or exhibited something which indicated some form of 'privileged' start in life. One memorable incident springs to mind: on the first morning of the three-day officer selection course at RAF Uxbridge, a gleaming Rolls Royce pulled up at the camp entrance and an elegantly and expensively dressed young man was ushered out of the vehicle by the chauffeur. The son of the chairman of one of Britain's largest construction companies had arrived to start his compulsory two year national Service. He walked through the camp to meet us, suitcase in hand and a broad, charming smile. The unease and deep resentment conveyed by the regular non-commissioned RAF staff was tangible.

This was my first experience of the so-called 'British disease' which seemed to be destroying the very foundations of the British motor industry. I went to some length to prevent this sort of attitude developing between staff and management at *Crayford.* One story circulating in the 1960s about the construction of a new car plant in Scotland seemed to sum up, in an extreme form, something of the essence of the prevailing problem. The first building to be completed and ready for occupation was the Communist Party Office, which had been constructed within the factory compound. Presumably it was a successful unit – within a few years production at the plant had discontinued and the factory had closed.

Years after starting up *Crayford,* someone suggested to me that the difference between a British car worker and his American counterpart could be summed up thus: when the Brit sees his boss arrive in a new Rolls Royce, his reaction is an angry: 'We'll get him out of that'. The American car worker, however, watching his boss arrive in a Cadillac, thinks: 'Nice, I'm gonna get one of those'. Having worked with both British and American workers, I believe there is some truth in this story. When I first drove up to our works in the finest car I have ever owned, a long wheel base V8 Mercedes, I was distinctly apprehensive about the workforce's reaction and perhaps that in itself says a good deal about the pervading atmosphere of the times. Even today, I imagine the sight of a boss in an expensive car still produces some unfortunate reactions in Britain.

Yet, unless we were in the midst of a crisis, I always tried to work on the factory floor from 8.00h until 11.00h. During my 25 years in convertible production, I tended to specialise on door and window work – always an area of technical difficulty. The two side windows on each side of a car present something of an engineering nightmare when the vehicle is turned into a convertible. The placing of glass in a vertical position without the support of a steel frame or surround, as in a saloon model, inevitably produces some engineering problems.

The principal difficulty centres on keeping the windows stiff enough to prevent them shaking when the car is travelling at speed on a rough surface, especially as the suspension is generally stiffer on high performance models. Another problem which can occur is when individuals lean their full weight on the glass, as if the vehicle were a saloon. I have often witnessed this at motor shows. The mechanisms – or regulators as they are called – which raise and lower the side windows into the bodywork frequently give trouble if abused and even if not. In 2004, for instance, I was forced to replace a regulator on my current VW Golf, with only 27,000 miles on the clock and I can say with absolute assurance that the vehicle had never been abused in any way.

Another difficulty which cropped up was with a *Crayford* Lotus Cortina when driven at well over 100 mph with the heater/cooler blower on its maximum, is that the windows and hood, which are already under considerable stress, get sucked outwards by the very aerodynamics of the vehicle shape. What we call laminar flow effect in fluid dynamics. Turning on the internal blower in such circumstances only compounds the problem. For this and other reasons, my area of speciality tended to focus on the window regulators – from tooling design and the ordering of parts to 'living' with the warranty problems and after-sales service, sometimes many years after the initial sale. Indeed, still today, the regulator problem remains an omni-present issue and I am currently overhauling the regulators which I installed on a Cortina 36 years ago.

My daily work pattern at *Crayford* was of necessity to a large extent given over to the administrative side of the business. Then, mid-afternoon I would put on my white coat again and return to the workshop floor where, like Jeff, I was at my happiest. I was also obeying what I believe to be the first rule in business: 'be there'. The pull of the engineering instincts went back into my family past. I always thought that my headmaster father would have made a great engineer, although he was also a gifted teacher. He enjoyed our early days, when Jeff and I went to Throwley House at Strood, spending many evenings working on our first Mini prototype and other projects. It was in his well-equipped garage there that I was able to indulge in my passion for engineering projects. When I was 16, he

*David liked to spend some time on the shop floor each day*

bought a second-hand six cylinder Vauxhall and one evening, during term time, he walked into his garage to find that I had almost taken the entire engine to pieces. Remarkably, he was very good about it and decided to leave me alone with the mighty task of putting it back together again.

I can recall another similar schooldays' escapade. Ernie Davies, my headmaster at King's School, Rochester, after the war somehow got hold of a complete new aeroplane engine, which I took to pieces in my continued need for exploration. He was good enough to take my adventure as a thirst for knowledge – after all, I was 16 at the time. The engineering trait was deep in the family background. My mother's father was an engineer in a large Belfast linen factory and as a small boy I can recall him reversing his Austin to the well outside their weekend cottage on the Antrim coast in Northern Ireland. Using the axle differential effect, he managed to drive a pump using one rear wheel to raise the water up to what was presumably a roof tank in the house. My grandfather on my father's side was a staunch Protestant lay preacher and sold religious books in Ulster. I inherited something of both traits, but ultimately the passion for engineering won through.

The one thing which exercised the greatest influence on my approach at *Crayford* was a management methods course I attended, run by a company called Coverdale and involving two courses over a period of six months. The ideas I picked up dramatically improved my effectiveness in running the business.

At the start of the course we were asked to write down the answers to a simple question that ran something along the lines of: why is making a profit in business important? A seemingly simple enough question, but the wide diversity of answers it produced from the 20 or so of us on the course came as quite a surprise. The message was then pressed home just how people can head off on different paths to answer the same question – with disastrous consequences for a company. The principle focus has to be one where, before you start looking for answers, the initial question or problem must be clearly analysed and defined. Then comes the next major step: to establish a success/failure criteria.

Using the Coverdale approach, and setting out criteria for success at the start of a project meant that I kept Jeff pinned to his seat on quite a few occasions, whilst we thrashed out just where we were heading on a particular project. Above all, this approach cleared the air, removing any differences of opinion and producing a specific aim: what we were going to do and, moreover, where and why we were going to do it. Using this method, we decided to develop two small cars as convertibles, the Ford Fiesta and the Mini Metro. In an inspired moment, I investigated the word 'Metro' and was astonished to discover that the manufacturer, British Leyland, had not bothered to register the world 'politan' or any other related Metro words, so we immediately had the name for our Metro convertible – the Metro Politan.

Developing the two cars simultaneously was a smart move, with Jeff leading the Metro team, while I focused on the Fiesta, giving rise to a sense of friendly rivalry and competition. From this work came a new approach. I had noticed that on the very old vehicles wood frequently outlasted steel on body parts and I had long concluded that the use of a hardwood such as ash was worth considering, especially in our case with low-volume production, a limited tooling budget and an accompanying need for quick alterations and modifications. So ash wood was used on several of the Fiesta conversion components.

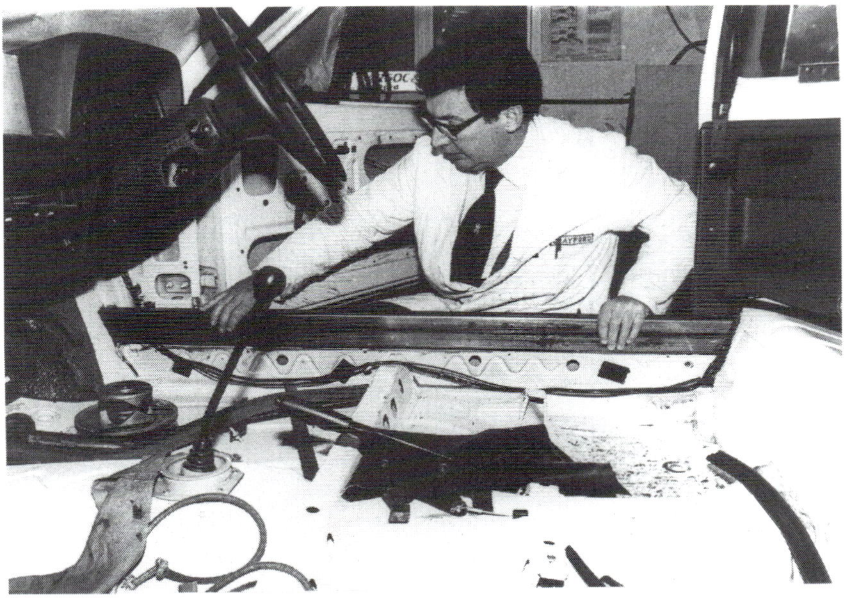

*David McMullan fits a Fiesta Fly sill*

We first used wood in the early sixties on the front header rails of the Mini convertible. Considerable benefits arose from this method when there was a slight change to the shape of the top of the windscreen – something you never heard about until it arrived or because our own welder had changed the angle of the jig. In this case, I could easily reshape the existing wooden pattern slightly, or even cut a new pattern in aluminium and then take it round to the carpentry workshop in Westerham to be made in hardwood.

This meant that I would have a new part in ash ready for use in no more than a few hours at virtually no cost, compared with those involved in normal manufacturing costs. Such flexibility is almost unthinkable in the case of steel components, although more recentdevelopments in the eighties in low-volume Kevlar plastic tooling have since changed the scene in this area of manufacture. By the Coverdale measure of targets and success or failure criteria, the Fiesta and Metro were both successfully completed on time.

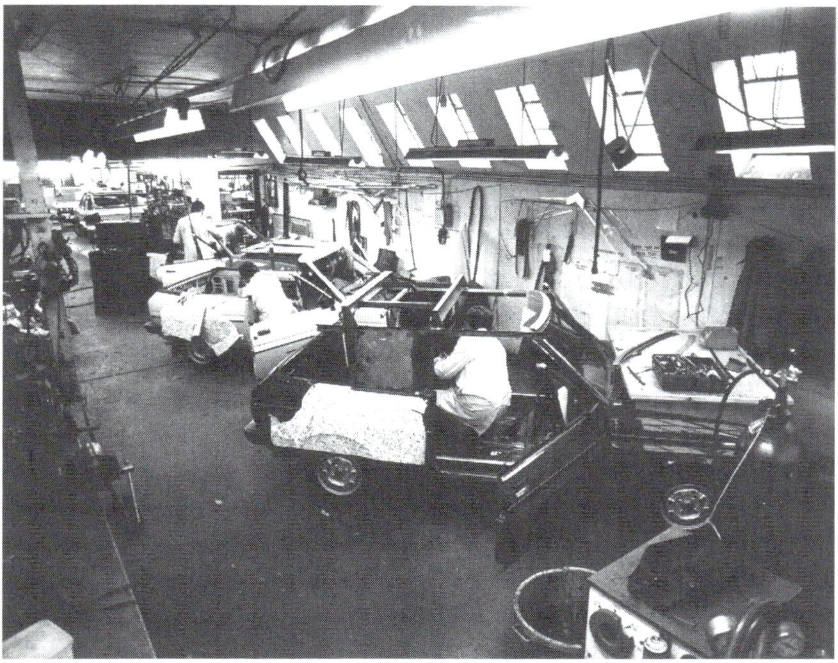

*Fiesta Fly in full production at Westerham*

From a management point of view I was slack about setting a realistic annual target for profitability, though I was aware of the need to be hugely profitable 'today' to absorb the R & D (research and development) costs of the products 'tomorrow'. If Jeff and his team spent three months on a project, for instance, this would clearly soak up profit in any given financial year.

Generally, the British Motor industry never seemed to grasp the basic essentials of a well-adjusted strategy for such circumstances. New engineering projects such as the Mini, rightly regarded by many as brilliant, were also in the opinion of some analysts a recipe for financial disaster, the problem being that the company never generated the huge and expensive budget surpluses so necessary for R & D, currency movements and totally 'out of the blue' disasters such as major model recalls to correct technical faults. I once saw an analysis of the profitability of the VW Beetle as opposed to the BL Mini. It seems that the Mini was really a non-starter as a long-term project. It didn't compare with the Beetle. I hope it now does.

I always had a personal management philosophy, I don't know where it came from, that there was absolutely no business problem that could not be solved, provided you threw enough money at it. It also applied in other walks of life, except health and love! Alan, a good friend in Ford Engineering said their philosophy was: 'We don't have problems, we have opportunities.' I liked that one too. Huge surplus profit is an absolute essential in my view and if you are not making it, watch out!

MG Rover seemed to have great problems generating enough profit in their final years before the company was sold. Similarly, it must have been a shattering experience for BMW to pour tens of millions of DM into the British Midlands motor industry, only to find that even they, a great and hugely successful German company, couldn't generate sufficient profit to cover the present commitments, let alone the all-important future requirements. The later success with the re-designed and larger Cowley-built Mini will hopefully make up for earlier problems.

So where do we look to find any form of 'magic' to account for the long-term success of Crayford during the almost total collapse of the British motor industry? It can perhaps be summed up in one simple example.

*Off with his head! A Mercedes Benz W123 conversion*

Daimler Benz Engineering headquarters at Sindelfingen in Germany received an instruction to supply a special long-wheelbase Grosse model Mercedes as a semi-convertible with electro-hydraulic mechanism in landaulet style. It was for the Premier of a Middle Eastern state. They had many options as to where to place the order and could easily have had it built 'in house'; it is common to let the apprentice division do 'one-offs' like this as an exercise. Or they could have placed it with one of Germany's excellent specialists such as Bauer or Deutsch. Another possibility would have been our friends

Chapron in Paris – or one of the multitude of very highly skilled American car design specialists.

In the event it was *Crayfords* who got the order. Perhaps because they knew us well, as the only manufacturers in the world to build the large Mercedes S Class Estate car and also the beautiful Crayford 280 Mercedes convertible. Maybe it was also because we were a fairly small company, who could work very quickly on new projects, but above all had two directors who got their hands dirty.

Chapter 18

# A Bend in the Road

My much-missed partner, Jeff, died nearly 30 years ago. An untimely death and a tragic one, which drastically altered the course of events for both me and the company, in a way that was unimaginable just a few years earlier. For Jeff, life had monumentally changed following the death, from cancer, of his wife Mary in 1970. He was not the same after that, his ever-present restlessness reaching new peaks. Thereafter he seemed to take extraordinary risks – almost as if he had lost his reason for living.

The fatal accident occurred in April 1985. He had travelled out to our villa in the village of Javea to return the British-registered BMW motorcycle we kept there. There was a good reason for bringing the bike back – the Spanish Police were well known for their habit of 'collecting' or even confiscating foreign-registered vehicles and then selling them off privately.

Whilst there, Jeff decided to go for a ride and deliver a bottle of whisky to an old friend, who lived just outside Javea and where the road narrows on a right-hand bend. She wasn't in, so he turned out of her driveway back towards Javea, but on the wrong side of the road – a mistake that is much more easily made on a motorcycle as it is not 'handed' like a car.

On the first left-hand bend he ran head-on into an oncoming car, which was moving so slowly that the elderly couple in the vehicle had quite expected to be able to help Jeff back onto his feet. But it was not to be. He probably died almost instantly.

Jeff had been driving without a crash helmet, having left it behind at his bedside at the villa – fatefully, he had lost one of the screws which held the chin piece in place. At least that was our theory at the time. In fact, the rest of the helmet was perfectly viable as an open face piece of protective headgear. It would almost certainly have saved his life. He was subsequently certified dead at Alicante Hospital.

A friend who had been with Jeff that day called me in Kent to report that he had disappeared. I then contacted friends at our insurance company in Denia and asked them to initiate a search by contacting local hospitals and police stations. It was a long and worrying day. Then, eventually, a call came from Denia. An unidentified motorcyclist had suffered a serious accident, but had not been carrying any documentation. However, the machine's registrations had been checked through the DVLA at Swansea and it belonged to *Crayford.*

The following day we received confirmation of his death. Everyone at *Crayford* was shattered by the news, especially my son Sean, then aged 18, who was in the office when the dreaded confirmation came through. Sean enjoyed a close relationship with his 'Uncle Jeffrey', a closeness that had developed because of his exceptional talent on the workshop floor and a quality that had very much appealed to Jeff.

At this stage, we were unclear about just what had happened. That evening Maureen agreed to fly out to Alicante to sort out matters and identify the body, which she duly did. Ironically, the day after Jeff's death was confirmed, our insurance broker accompanied by an area insurance representative, arrived to advise us of a massive increase in our insurance premiums as a result of Jeff's various motorcycle and car accidents and other circumstances in the insurance industry. I sent them packing.

Everyone connected with Crayford was absolutely devastated and the effect on me personally is difficult to surmise even today. There was, however, great support at hand. Maureen, in particular, was a tower of strength, especially now that she had given up medicine and had retrained as a secretary. She was a wonderful partner and able to move in immediately to take on the business at hand with commanding assurance.

Then there was Eugene Dunn, who had worked with us at Lambretta Trojan in the 1960s and had offered to move in straight away and help me. And Sally, our secretary who knew the business inside out, offering boundless help and support. Of course, there were difficulties, how to handle future research and development projects, a field in which Jeff had always taken the lead, though in truth we had always worked at it together. I would set the parameters – just how many weeks I considered I could afford to 'lose' him while he buried himself at the far end of the works with one or two technicians. This had enabled me to carry on with the rest of business whilst he worked his magic. If left alone in this way, Jeff could produce a complete prototype, with initial tooling and pattern work, within a matter of eight weeks.

By this stage, the *Crayford* business, was well diversified. Throughout the 1970s we had been developing the ATV Argocat business, which had been going from strength to strength. We held the distribution rights throughout Europe, as well as in one or two other areas. The specialist equipment for inshore amphibious treatment of oil slicks was also very successful and due entirely to Jeff's development project in that field. Kent County Council used some of the vehicles and co-operation was excellent. Because of its amphibious nature, the machine developed by Jeff could spray oil slicks on inshore waters and also climb over the rocks, still spraying the detergent while it was at the same time working on the beaches.

For the 12 months following Jeff's death, I went around in a daze, struggling to run the business, maintain all the overseas contacts and also work on future projects. But I was fortunate in that, after the initial shock, the staff overcame the loss and were totally loyal. Anything I wanted, was done. I was lucky, too, that in the 1980s Britain was forging ahead in many areas except, that is, the motor industry. And here *Crayford* was almost unique, making profits. At the time of the tragedy, in 1985, we didn't actually have any new highly complex R & D programmes in hand, other than our continuing experimentation with the diesel engined, hydrostatically driven Argo.

Maureen my wife was a wonderful helper at that difficult time and we had some amusing moments together. One Friday morning the phone rang in an outer office. Maureen, who had a similar voice to one of our lady staff members, happened to be walking past, answered it then put it down and came into my office with one eyebrow raised which she always did when something very amusing happened. She said, "A gentleman from Ford Engineering Essex has just been on the phone. He said I am to get my knickers off as he's on his way over …" The gentleman concerned was used to a Friday inspection visit at Crayfords to see how were getting on with the latest secret Ford prototype, enjoy a lunchtime pint and had, it appears, established a friendly relationship with a young lady staff member. Moments like this helped to lighten the atmosphere after losing Jeffrey.

There was, however, one nightmare on the insurance front. During the six to eight months prior to Jeff's death, we had been working on a policy to protect us in the future against various 'unforeseens', including sudden death or disability, both of which would have had serious repercussions on the company. There was a standing joke that we shared: whoever came off his motorbike first and ended up in a wheelchair would have to be pushed by the other up the ramp to the chassis installation shop, the implication being that this was why it was there. It was not, of course: the chassis shop lay on a different level to the main workshop and factory.

To cover ourselves for all eventualities I had prepared an insurance policy to encompass everything, including a massive sum to enable the surviving partner, if necessary, to buy the other's shareholding in the company. The forms had been completed and I had had the required medical. They then sat on my desk for months. Jeff's forms lay on the other side of the desk and in all likelihood he had used them as a coffee mat. Every month or so I would raise the vexed issue and urge him to sign the forms.

A couple of days before he was due to fly out to Spain on that ill-fated weekend, I pressed home the point yet again. He agreed to do it that Thursday, but then he realised he needed a medical and phoned 'Mosey' (his pet name for my wife) and asked her to carry out the examination. She agreed, urging him to go straight up to our house in Tatsfield. He then called our insurance brokers in Crowborough, Sussex, and explained what he was going to do. But they pointed out that my wife was not on their approved list and that only a handful of doctors in the London area were authorised to carry out such examinations. However, an appointment could be arranged for him on that Thursday. This did not appeal to Jeff, having to fly to Spain the following day, and as a result he didn't sign the forms and failed to have the medical. He was killed that weekend, uninsured.

A nightmare scenario then opened up before me. Our accountants and solicitors explained that, legally, Jeff's shares – 50% of the company – had to be put on the market and sold swiftly, properly and transparently. An immediate threat loomed. I was aware that a firm in northern France was building a similar ATV vehicle and would have their sights on our company. I was convinced that, within a few weeks I would lose half of *Crayford* and, no doubt, soon be levered out of the company. Somehow, I had to scratch together every penny I could possibly lay my hands on to avoid this happening and buy Jeff's share myself. I had, in fact, been saving for years and so, with the cooperation of the bank and others, I managed to gather together the necessary funds to buy the other half of the company and thus carry on trading

Whilst trying to resolve all these financial issues, yet another unexpected legacy of problems arose from Jeff's will, which he had drawn up four years previously. He had left clear instructions that everything he owned was to go to his children, Catherine and Richard, then aged 17 and 19 years. Jeff and I had long had a mutual understanding, based on total trust, that in the event of one of us dying, each would carry out the other's instructions to the letter.

The new situation placed me in an extraordinarily difficult position – confronting his partner (and my friend) with whom he had shared his life and who had run his home for many years, with the news that she had been left absolutely nothing. I was presented with a very painful and emotional dilemma. She was his 'wife', having replaced, as far as anyone could, Mary. In an attempt to solve this – and to share the grief over Jeff's death – I met my great friend, Ian Williams. Explaining how I felt trapped by circumstances, his advice remains with me to this day. 'Listen', he said, 'Jeffrey's gone and, as far as we know, he is not coming back. So it's your job to sort it out as best you can. Just get on with it.' I did just that.

Jeff's death left me to reflect on his press-on characteristics, personality traits which came to the fore after the devastating experience of his wife Mary's death. But that irrepressible driving spirit had been with him for most of his life. He often recalled to me his early motorcycling escapades around his home village of Talybont in South Wales and how, on one occasion, he found his father standing in the doorway of the family home, waiting for him. Jeff decided to put on a brief motorcycle handling demonstration for his father, 'blipping' the bike so that he could throw the front wheel up onto the pavement, to be followed by the back wheel, and then coming to a halt at the front door. As luck would have it, the manoeuvre went awry and his Gold Star BSA finally crashed to the ground and ended up close to his father's feet. Mr. Smith senior was unamused. He looked down at his son lying beneath the bike and then simply stepped inside the house and quietly closed the door. The incident apparently summed up their relationship. I also heard a rumour that on one occasion he actually levelled a twelve-bore gun at his father. A friend in Majorca told me recently that it was highly likely that there was some female involvement. Jeffrey was very active socially during his early years.

Lovely man though he was, Jeff was difficult to get on with at times; determined and driven, yet fun to work with, unless things went wrong in the workshop. On several occasions over the years I was confronted by an angry and frightened member of staff, who would claim that a hammer or some other tool had been hurled across the workshop and buried itself in the opposite wall. That was the telltale sign of Jeff's frustration, particularly evident in later years when his eyesight was no longer all that it might have been and he had to resort to wearing glasses and found it difficult to identify the actual size of a drill or, on his back underneath the front bulkhead of a car, whilst trying to sort out wiring or other detailed problem.

He was perhaps one of the last of the instinctive hands-on development engineers in the motor industry. His background was essentially practical, much of it having been learnt during his early training years back in the Talybont village garage. His suspicion of computers and their contribution to business or engineering in the early days was well-founded, but times have moved on and the era of the in-demand computer engineer had arrived.

Twenty years after Jeff's death, Ian Williams – the man who had brought the young engineer from South Wales and introduced him to me at Lambretta Trojan – invited me over to Majorca for a long lunch to celebrate the memory of our departed friend. The Spanish restaurant owners must have been puzzled by our behaviour, for we kept a spare seat at the table, to which Ian would occasionally address an admonition, declaring in no uncertain terms what he thought of Jeff's action in leaving us all too early. The inspired and inspirational engineer, for whom 'enough was just not good enough' was no 'pussy cat' and is still sadly missed by many.

*Ian Williams and David Mc Mullan hold a memorial lunch in Palma twenty years after the death of Jeff Smith*

It was a cruel irony that the BMW machine which he so much enjoyed riding had cost him his life and in such seemingly simple and mundane circumstances. It was fitting tribute to him, though, that the day after we had attended his funeral in Brecon in 1985, the Crayford Owners Club put on show the Mini convertible AFO 887, our first conversion (completed in 1962 and based on a second-hand vehicle supplied by Jeffrey's brother-in-law's Central Garage in Brecon) at the Classic Car Show.

One of the last sombre tasks I gave myself before selling off

*Crayford* was to make a stainless steel plate with Jeff's name inscribed on it, involving a touch of poignant symbolism. I cut his name into the plate using the special air-powered blaster we had always used to clean up a chassis before painting. Two years had elapsed since his death, yet I still found cutting that plate a painful and upsetting business. Standing at the bench in the lower workshop in the Westerham factory, almost furtively filing and cutting, I was hoping that no-one would notice the tears in my eyes. Almost as an instinctive afterthought, I then etched in four initials – one in each corner of this small memorial plaque: *D* for David, *M* for Maureen, *I* for Ian Williams and *H* for Helmut Heine – the latter being the managing director of the Canadian ODG company, who had become a close friend of ours. I then took the plaque to Spain and fixed it into the stone wall on the bend where Jeff had died.

It was in part a moving tribute to Jeff – whose talents as a gifted engineer were widely recognised – that after his death so many people came in to offer support and assistance, among them Ian Williams and Sally, our secretary, who was a pillar of strength in difficult times. Also Maureen, who by then had decided she had had enough of life as a GP and the world of medicine and, under a Government scheme, had re-trained as a secretary to help me at the works. In doing so she also brought with her the always highly valued skills of a trained doctor, tending professionally to the usual range of wounds and injuries sustained in the chassis shop. Her easy-going presence was an added bonus and appreciated by the staff, men and women alike.

Inevitably, the two years following Jeff's death brought huge pressures for me. I was by then bearing the full burden of running the company, including the new responsibilities for factory floor problems and issues of basic engineering and development. There was now the added responsibility for forward product development, an area in which Jeff excelled, once I had sown the initial seed. I continued, too, following my personal rule of spending three to four hours each morning on the factory floor, tools in hand and in my overalls, trying to keep up-to-date and on top of everything happening in the technical area.

In 1986, at the instigation of Helmut Heine, we paid a visit to Jeff's grave in Wales, accompanied by our wives. Helmut had sensed just how devastated I was by the death of my best friend and business partner, although at that point the company's prospects were distinctly encouraging – both turnover and profits were up and staff morale excellent.

I can recall sitting on the edge of the bed in our hotel room in Brecon and turning to Maureen to say: 'Helmut made a really strange comment. He asked me whether I had thought of retiring'. Maureen responded simply: 'Well, if you don't, you are going to die quite young'. Her remark hit me like a hammerblow, as intended. Such a prognosis from my wife was that of an experienced doctor, a 'tough love' message. It was time to pay attention. The seeds of change had been sown.

# Chapter 19

# The Sale of Crayford

I had suspected that I would be quite good at the business of selling *Crayford*, putting together the sales document and identifying exactly what was for sale and where potential problems might arise. Although I had never before prepared anything of this nature, my earlier school experience at King's, Rochester, had given me the confidence about my ability to set down my thoughts and ideas. One classroom scene had remained with me: Ian Newman, Head of English, walking to the back of the class, where I used to hide, and handing back our essays with the remark: 'It's good to know that I am not wasting my time'. My paper was marked 'A'. A similarly encouraging response had occurred in the sixth form. I had been instructed to prepare an essay on Chaucer, but instead for some reason chose to spend my summer holiday researching the history of anaesthetics. The resulting essay on the subject nonetheless won a reassuring nod of approval from the master.

Shortly after the trip to Wales in 1986, I gave an Argocat demonstration near Helsinki in Finland. After the initial hour discussing and demonstrating the vehicle's capabilities in and out of a nearby river, the convivial host firm threw an impromptu party. It was 11.00 am but they were eager for me to sample the various types of schnapps. At that time of the morning such a liquor intake on an empty stomach hit my system like undiluted 'firewater'. Further surprises were to follow. At lunchtime, I was led to a clearing in the forest, where incredibly a dartboard had been fixed to a tree. The assumption was that all Englishmen played darts and my hosts were keen to witness an expert demonstration. But, by that point, I could see multiple dartboards rather than just the one. Nonetheless, by focusing on the 'middle target' I somehow managed to give an acceptable enough demonstration of the noble art of English dart throwing while under the influence. That evening, in my hotel bedroom in Helsinki, was one that will stay with me. It was then that, with a feeling of deep sadness, I first sat down with a few sheets of paper to prepare a draft for the sales brochure which would effectively get rid of my company – and my life's work.

Back in Kent, I met my accountant Ian MacDonald in our favourite lunchtime pub, the Chafford Arms near Tunbridge Wells, and I told him of my plan to sell. Following several subsequent meetings, he and his partner Jim Thompson came up with a value for the company that was considered reasonable, yet not too ambitious – I was anxious to keep the freehold of the factory premises in Westerham. Meetings with friends and associates followed until Peter Agg, my old boss from the Lambretta Trojan days, urged me to change to one of the big London accountancy companies, with departments specialising in placing businesses for sale and, equally important, with specialist knowledge of the tax liabilities which might accrue from such a deal. His advice was invaluable and Ian MacDonald took this change of plan in good spirit, being totally supportive. There were no hard feelings.

I then visited the prestigious City firm of Deloittes for a meeting which, memorably for me, took place in a magnificent conference room. I suppose I must have been a shade overawed by the surroundings, as I sat in silence while no less than 12 company officials – complete strangers to me – inspected my sales figures, scoured my brochure and accounts and chatted amongst themselves. Eventually, the chairman of the meeting asked me how much I wanted for the company. Instinctively, I decided to stick another £50,000 onto the figure Ian MacDonald had first agreed. Silence followed. Had I overpriced the company? Even worse, had I dropped a 'clanger'?

With undisguised embarrassment, the chairman peered over his glasses and said quietly, 'We should comfortably double that figure'. His response threw me completely. Treading uncertainly in strange and unknown financial territory, I was patently getting things terribly wrong. Then I was informed that they had about 20 possible buyers for an engineering company of my type of profitability and, further, they were unlikely to need to go down that list beyond the first one or two potential buyers. However, what they needed to do was to produce a sales brochure of their own, a book almost, designed to enable a potential buyer to examine, in the comfort of an armchair, the past, present, and possible future prospects of the business.

An agreeably pleasant young New Zealander accountant was then despatched to Kent to shadow me for a week. Each evening he would return to my house in Tatsfield to question me further about detailed issues. The resulting 'book', which cost £3000 to produce, frankly baffled me and large chunks, in particular the graphs and statistics on the company's future prospects, were almost beyond my understanding. At one point in the Deloitte meetings, I was introduced to a young lady who was charged with responsibility for 'number-crunching' whatever that meant. She was nice.

It was instructive to discover how a large and thorough organisation such as Deloittes went about the business of trying to assess the future prospects of a company such as ours. Instructive too, because it was clear that the auditing house could not possess an intimate and close knowledge of my sort of business. Self-evident questions emerged time and again: how, for example, could or would Deloittes know if someone in Japan had started to build a copy of the Argocat using a new differential system that Honda had developed, in an operation that could conceivably put a halt to our business overnight? These were highly technical issues, calling for years of knowledge and experience to assess and yet they were matters which could have a crucial bearing on a company's future prospects and profitability potential. So I was left reflecting and pondering quite how anyone, lacking the specialist knowledge acquired by someone like myself over many years of practical involvement and a close scrutiny of the ever-shifting changes occurring within our industry, could even begin to make detailed assessments concerning long-term business potential.

The same sort of questions and ideas occurred to me again, years later, when following my retirement from *Crayford*, I was working for Oxfam in African countries. Even the brightest African technician seldom possessed the in-depth technical knowledge and background that is to be found in Europe – a vast area of knowledge, covering everything from motorcycles to generators and aircraft.

This is what we might call the European technical inheritance, the invaluable store of knowledge and experience handed down through generations. Something of that inherent skill factor may have applied in the case of my family: my schoolteacher father, the natural engineer and my grandfather an outstanding one. Some of that must have rubbed off on me. It's the old nurture/nature conundrum.

Despite my misgivings, the rapidly assembled Deloittes brochure instantly worked. I was worried, however, about the unsettling effect sale negotiations and enquiries might have on the workforce, so I insisted that the first potential buyer to show interest should visit me in the evening and then examine the books further over several successive evenings. One London stockbroker acquaintance asked me if he could mention the sale to one of his clients. I didn't have any exclusivity deal with Deloittes and so the suggested enquiry went ahead. The prospective purchasers were David Connold, who then owned a main General Motors franchise and his partner David Butlion, a director at GM Luton.

David Connold first chatted with me about a possible deal for a couple of hours at my Tatsfield home. After a while, I invited him to share a glass of Spanish red wine, standing on a shelf, a left-over from Christmas. As he sipped the wine, I asked what he thought of it. 'Well, it's OK', he replied, 'as long as you don't get any of it on your skin!' I immediately thought 'he's my man'.

During a further furtive meeting, Connold introduced me to his partner, the other David. They offered to move quickly if I suspended negotiations with Deloittes. For me that didn't present a problem, not having been too impressed with the potential buyers they had sent down to see us in Kent. So the meetings with the two Davids continued. My secretary, Sally, as alert and sharp as ever, soon discovered what was going on though.

Inevitably it was a testing and trying time and it was just at this point that Maureen truly came into her own. She was by now combining a number of roles, most admirably as always – looking after the home, helping me at the factory and caring for our second son, Sean, as he prepared to set off alone, with little money in his pocket, to try his luck 'testing his wings' in America. Yet, amidst all this, she still somehow found time to sit in on the meetings with the, by now, 'three Davids', the potential buyers and myself.

I welcomed the extra support she brought to the negotiating table and it was clear that the two purchasing executives were acutely aware that at my side was a wife and business associate who possessed a first-class mind and, crucially, a phenomenal memory. As in all negotiations, there were some sticky moments, when both sides pushed the boundaries to test just where, in truth, we all stood. Maureen's qualities came truly to the fore when, after a two-week gap in negotiations, we became locked in a disagreement on a minor point.

Connold and Butlion disagreed with my interpretation of what I thought they had set out two weeks previously. Maureen, however, brought matters swiftly and succinctly to a head, by repeating word for word, just what they had said a fortnight earlier. That settled the matter – almost in an instant. Her powers of recall were remarkable and of incalculable help in these friendly, yet delicately argued, negotiations.

As the sale discussions dragged on – as they were bound to do – the buyer duo and I got both to know and trust each other. They were nice, agreeable individuals and no trouble to work with. We visited Aird Motors at Beauly in Scotland – by far our best Argocat distributor, to inform them about the projected *Crayford* handover.The Airds manager, David Anderson, and his wife Christine, entertained us royally and after a lot of whisky we returned to Inverness Airport for the return journey. As it turned out, we had missed our flight, so returned to the city and the partying continued. A close relationship had been established. Once again I left Inverness, as so often before, not really feeling too well.

Later we travelled together to Ontario, to inform the ODG executives all about the plan and convince them that, in the new company format, *Crayford* would remain the best agents to represent the Argocat in Europe. Butlion and Connold were impressive men with a great deal of experience, one with General Motors contacts worldwide, the other a Vauxhall main dealer with extensive contacts in Britain and a deep knowledge of the motor trade. More than that, they were offering an improved contract with ODG, greater management strength and better funding.

Back in Westerham, David Butlion continued to shadow me, thus learning all about the business just as quickly as he could. A good deal of time was spent negotiating the value of the stock they were taking over, always a potential problem area in a business sale.The spare parts inventory, for example, might suggest that it is sensible to keep some 100 tyres in stock, but perhaps only 50 gearbox casings, for the simple reason that only two of the latter may sell in the course of a year. Moreover, it was difficult to gauge in advance what the failure rate might be when new engine types with higher torque came onto the market. For this and other imponderables, many of our stock valuations went through 'on the nod', reflecting the spirit of 'give and take' that was displayed by both sides.

Last minute alterations were made as the final contract was drawn up during an overlong and exhausting meeting in London, which continued into the early hours. By then I had discovered that there is a standard on-line computer contract which covers almost every facet of selling a business, which could have saved me a lot of time. Finally, there was some wheeling and dealing, followed by the insertion of names and sums of money. There was one clause, however, for which I was totally unprepared: the stipulation which prohibited me from any involvement in vehicle design for the following ten years, a condition designed to ensure that I wouldn't set up another business in competition. After all, at that stage in my life I possessed all the necessary contacts and know-how to do just that.

What a strange sensation completing the contract at 03.00h, in the wee hours of the morning. Maureen wasn't with me and I was feeling very alone and forlorn as I wandered through the back streets of West London, walking from the solicitor's office to collect my car at the Victoria Station vehicle park. I just sat for a while in my big 'S' class Mercedes and reflected on the changes the sale would bring to my life, not least to my lifestyle – the prospect, for one thing, of being unable to afford a top of the range Mercedes, amongst other such hard-earned luxuries.

A memorable farewell party followed at the well-known half-timbered Grasshopper pub on the A25, just outside Westerham. All the factory staff and our *Crayford* friends were invited. A delightful surprise awaited me – a montage *(see opposite)* featuring some of the more memorable and humorous incidents which had occurred at *Crayford* over the years. It still hangs on the wall of my home in Javea to remind me of past adventures and ventures: a photograph of the axle assembly sitting in the corner of Maureen's maternity ward, the week our first son Peter was born; a photo of a customer arriving at our offices with a warranty claim and, the happiest of images, a photograph of camels in the desert to remind us of a 3-month, 12,000 mile expedition across the Sahara and North Africa in 1974 by Land Rover with the family on board,

Looking back now on that all-important change to my life in 1987, I can count myself lucky. The new owners were good people with whom to conduct business. We never had any serious or protracted arguments on any issue before, during or after the sale of *Crayford.* Given the sums of money involved, that was some achievement. I had sold the company with ease, helped no doubt by the prevailing economic conditions. During the mid-to-late 80s, the British economy was buoyant and surging ahead, creating a financial climate in which it was relatively easy to dispose of what was, in this case, a 'healthy business baby'.

Another significant contributing factor, which helped to make this transaction as satisfactory as it was smooth, was the fact that from the very beginning, in 1962, I had followed the practice of producing a monthly no-holds-barred analysis of our true financial position. At times this could be a ruthlessly revealing cost-accounting experience. We might have spent thousands of pounds and yet still only be at the half-way stage in the development of a new car project. Especially unnerving too if, for some reason, the business would have had to be sold at that point, in which case all the costly jigs and special tools

*Montage (from top right, clockwise):*

*1. Mercedes estate seats folded flat – providing 'relaxation facilities' late at night during Crayford works' parties*

*2. Amphibious experimental Fiesta: Jeffrey has to exit by window as the doors are welded*

*3. Toilet door blown open after propane is fed under the door and then ignited: staff most amused, but Jeffrey wasn't*

*4. Unlucky Arab owner of new bullet-proofed Crayford Mercedes is assassinated*

*5. 1974 McMullan family using Crayford converted Land Rover with long range tanks fitted to cross the Sahara and central Africa*

*6. (bottom left) Hospital bed and birth of young Peter McMullan in 1962 with a customer carrying an axle and a warranty claim having confused Dr Maureen McMullan with David McMullan*

*7. Red and blue petrol cans: the bosses David and Jeffrey used to steal each other's cans, to the great amusement of the staff*

*8. Jan, our Indian cook, prepared regular Friday afternoon curry parties*

*9. Some famous Crayford customers including Rolf Harris, Sofia Loren and Dean Martin*

would be rendered totally valueless.

Performing this exercise, year in year out, keep us profitable. Of that I am quite sure. It was often a stunning experience to watch just how quickly, totally without warning, the company could swing from extreme profitability to merely breaking even. I clearly recall the reaction of the 'two Davids', when I threw the relevant documents down on to the negotiating table. They were stunned into silence. Before them were records of all the day-to-day financial matters, reaching back to the earliest point in my operations, when I possessed no facilities and simply used my father's Gestetner duplicating machine at Throwley House to print off my documents. I continued with this system right through until 1987 and the sale of the business. There were few comparable companies in the UK motor engineering trade capable of producing such a volume of detailed paperwork and a sequence of accounts showing a profit on operations virtually throughout the entire twenty-five year life of the business.

The spirit of *Crayford* was revived for me – and in a most gratifying way to mark my 70th birthday in 2002. Through the efforts of my sons, Peter and Sean, I was reunited with one of the classic cars we had built in the late 1960s – a Cortina Convertible. The owner, a Californian businessman, who operates a specialised car rental service for the US film industry, happened to stumble across Crayford Coachworks, the Los Angeles company run by my sons. He was aware that the vehicle had been built by us in Westerham and asked if there was a business connection between *Crayford* and Crayford Coachworks. The boys were delighted to then fill him in about the background and connection between the two companies. After overhauling the Cortina for an appearance in an Austin Powers film, Sean and Peter bought it and had it shipped over to England. It finally arrived in the UK in 2004, registration RKL 700G.

Donna and I then drove it from Kent down to Javea. The drive went without a hitch, despite the ever-nagging fear that the cooling system on the 36 year-old Ford engine, with 90,000 miles on the clock, would wilt in the heat of a Spanish summer.

It seems more than likely that this was the same vehicle we had shown at the Chicago Motor Show in 1968 and its re-discovery triggered a remarkable sequence of coincidences and surprises. A matchbox bearing the logo of a Chicago hotel was found under the boot mat. Then, when the number plates were removed, the original UK registration plates were found still in place.

But there was still a final surprise waiting for us. The Crayford Convertible Car Club uncovered a photograph of a white Cortina Convertible bearing the same English number plate. The photo had been taken in 1968 – no doubt before its shipment to the US – in a car park at The Grasshopper, a short distance along the A25 from our factory in Westerham. This was the very same pub where in 1987 I had made my emotional farewells to *Crayford*, and all that the company meant to me.

*Reunited with the Cortina Convertible: the famous Chicago Show car that surfaced in California many years later .*

# Chapter 20

# Departure and Advice

If anyone had told me in 1960 that one day there would be a motoring magazine (*Crayview*), published regularly in England about the business I had created, I would have found it inconceivable. But the *Crayview* magazine has been published regularly by Barry Priestman and his helpers since 1981 and distributed to the Crayford Club members all over the world. I have to say it is a source of great pleasure for me to know that the products that Jeffrey and I developed over the years are now highly valued.

The year 1987 saw my departure from England and the handover of the factory keys. Maureen and I did not particularly want to leave England, but the tax system made retirement in England unacceptably expensive. It seemed madness to me that I could easily avoid a huge tax bill by living abroad and investing my money outside Britain in, say, a French motor manufacturer, but not in a British company. I hope this madness no longer exists. My financial advisors told me that there was no way round it.

Before leaving England, I was to receive further financial advice. I had a call from a Welshman, for whom we had built two really special Mercedes 280 CE convertibles some time ago. He had become a close friend of Jeffrey's. When he heard that I was selling *Crayford* and retiring, he suggested we meet for lunch somewhere between Kent and Cardiff, which we did.

He knew I was about to receive quite a large sum of money after the sale of the Company. After a chatty lunch, I can clearly remember he pushed the plates out of the way, as if to 'clear the deck' for action. Then he said, very slowly and clearly… roughly as follows:

'David, you have for 25 years been successful in one of the toughest industries, the motor industry and you think you have dealt with some pretty slick and devious people. However, you are shortly going to be approached by a bunch of highly-skilled professionals, who will probably run rings around you. They have been expertly trained to transfer as much money as possible, in the form of "commissions", from your bank account to theirs.

They are called "financial consultants" or "investment advisors" and are up to just about every trick in the book. Be wary, especially if their business is not properly registered as a Limited or SL Company, or if they do not hold a proper UK accountants qualification, or if their "head office" is, for some peculiar reason, based well away from the UK in, say, Cyprus or the Caribbean.'

How I wish I had paid more attention to what that Welshman said that day.

The tax regulations required us to leave England and so Maureen and I finally drove to Spain in April 1987, after a three-day wait in the Calais George V Hotel for our new Jaguar, which had broken down in Bromley. We had to wait for it to be sent across the Channel.

We drove first to Switzerland, so that I could examine some Argo spares on behalf of the new *Crayford* owners. It was a pleasant start to the retirement we were both looking forward to. Before long, however, I was to be totally devastated by Maureen's sudden death. She had surrendered to an almost unbeatable addiction.

The *Crayford* story was over, for me anyway. I had lost Mary, Jeffrey and Maureen. None had even reached 60.

I threw myself into a second career, as an overseas Oxfam engineer and a few years later, another truly wonderful woman, Donna, came into my shattered life and helped me slowly put it back together.

Jeff Smiths children Cath and Rick have settled with their families in Kent and have no motor industry connection .

Crayford's name however continues in California as "Crayford Paintless Dent Repair". This is run by Sean and is well known for its quality and inventiveness. Peter manages a successful auto-collision repair facilty and Sarah Jane is involved in international sales of exotic rare cars in Los Angeles .

*A Crayford Allegro convertible*

*The Crayford Mercedes 600 convertible*

# History of Crayford

Compiled by The Crayford Convertible Car Club

## Part I

**1959/60** – David McMullan (Sales Manager) and Jeff Smith (R & D) were working together at Lambretta-Trojan in Croydon, South London, on various Lambretta projects. They then worked even more closely under the supervision of the Group Chief Engineer, Ian Williams, on Kart racing projects. Finally they were both closely involved in the development of the Elva Courier sportscar at Lambretta Trojan

**1961** – It was during this time at Lambretta that Jeff and David formed a lifelong friendship and working partnership. They also shared a dream to produce a car of their own making. The revolutionary new Mini was still new and the dream was to produce the world's first convertible Mini. Unable to afford a new car they started work on a 1959-registered car, AFO 887, supplied by Jeff's family's garage in Brecon, Wales.

They worked by day at Lambretta, and in the evening in the garage of David's father at Throwley House, Strood. David had a flat at Bexleyheath and the telephone was on the Crayford exchange. Answering the phone with the word Crayford, the name stuck and so Crayford became the name of their as yet unborn company. By the end of 1961 the convertible Mini AFO 887 was completed, the very same night that David's first child, Peter, was born.

**1962** – David and Jeff moved both families to Tatsfield near Westerham in Kent. David and his wife, Maureen, borrowed £40 for tools from Barclays Bank at Bexleyheath.

**1963** – June 3rd, Crayford launch the Mini convertible to the world in the national press. It cost just £129 to convert, if you supplied the car. David and Jeff gave up their day jobs to set up on their own as Crayford Auto Developments, with a toolbox each and a joint investment of £20

**1964** – Crayford Mini sales boomed and an Autocar advert shows a UK dealership of 16 approved Crayford Mini agents, including one in Jersey. Crayford set up a system with dealers supplying customers with new saloons for conversion. Crayford kept capital outlay minimal, and held monthly audits. This system stood them in good stead over the next 20 years.

**1964** – Crayford Mini production was set up in Australia under Licence by Birchwood Motors in Victoria.

**1964** – Crayford Cortina Mk.1 was launched at the Racing Car Show at Olympia, London. Thirty were ordered as a taxi hire fleet for the Island of Bermuda. A further 17 also sold before the Mk.1 model ends.

**1965** – Crayford launched the Ford Corsair convertible for £325, to many it will be the best looking of all the Crayford conversions. Over 100 convertibles and 19 cabriolets being sold. Carl Deutsch in Germany built all the cabriolets.

**1965** – The giant Heinz 57 Food Company (Ltd) asked for 57

Mini convertibles to give away as prizes in a soup competition, in a secret deal with the Heinz directors at a greasy spoon café in Biggin Hill. They secured a deal around 57 Wolseley conversions to keep the cars unique to Heinz, with no copies, and a year's delay in the competition launch to give Crayford time to build all the prize cars. Crayford appointed Wigley engineering of Leatherhead to decapitate the cars and each car was then finished and trimmed at Jeff and David's homes in Tatsfield.

BMC 1100 Estate conversion launched for new and used cars from £79–£115 (deluxe). This was a UK first and preceded a factory 11/1300 estate.

## Part II

**1966** – Heinz gave away the 57 prize convertibles in a long summer of individual and group giveaways, surrounded by lots of press. The payment from Heinz for 57 cars provided the funding for the deposit to buy the Crayford factory in Westerham. A proposed deal to buy the site of Westerham Railway Station, recently axed by Dr.Beeching, fell through. But then they settled on purchasing The Old Printing Works, Westerham, complete with attached cottage, which became the new Crayford factory. The name *Crayford Auto Development Ltd* was registered. Soon they would be recognised worldwide as *Crayford of Westerham* .

The Austin/Morris 1800 (landcrab) 5 Door Hatchback Estate launched at £115. It became one of the company's longest best sellers. The Landcrab 1800 had a Production run of 11 years and the Crayford estate versions, which cost £1000 in tooling the rear conversion, was Britain's first successful large hatchback.

The new Cortina Mk.2 Convertible was launched on 19th Oct at Crayford's first International Motor Show at Earls Court,

London. This was only two weeks after Ford had launched the Mk.2 saloon range. Jeff Smith had worked night and day for two weeks, not only converting the car, but also taking it to GT spec from a bare shell, as Ford had no spare 2 door GT cars before the launch. The conversion cost from £325 and a Lotus convertible was also available. Selling over 400 units, it was Crayford's best seller, along with 400 Mk.3 Cortinas. The Cortina was the company bread and butter car for 20 years.

**1967** – Rover 2000/V8 P6 Estate launched and marketed by Crayford. Of the total 400 made, they sold the first 100 as Crayford's. This was a Crayford design and built by FLM Panelcraft's Fulham based works.

**1968** – Crayford Vauxhall Viva HB Cabriolet launched with Wallace Arnold as main agent. David Mc.Mullan's wife was asked to buy the all new saloon donor car for the prototype cabriolet. As a working doctor, she alone had the funds.

**1969** – Crayford launched the Capri convertible, called the Caprice, based on the all new Capri Mk.1, the car you always promised yourself. Crayford sold over 35 units. They had some direct competition as Abbott's of Farnham made and sold 9 convertible Capri cars and Carbodies built 2 Capri's with power hoods for Ford to evaluate. They then dumped the cars, as unprofitable to build in volume.

Crayford BMC1300 Cabriolet launched for Kent BMC dealers Caffyn's who had a branch at Westerham next to the Crayford Factory. A complex re-design of a hatchback into a convertible, it cost from £1,519 and only 12 were sold.

The 'Exterminator' a 4.7 Litre V8 Capri Saloon Q-car was shown at the Earls Court Motor Show. Orders for 30 for one delivery to Spain were taken, the same client also importing many V6 engined Mk.2 Cortina saloons.

Crayford launched the M/Benz114 'Compact' Estate. A

Crayford design built with some FLM Panelcraft of Fulham development. M/Benz took legal action to ban an all M/Benz Estate stand for the 1970 Earls Court Motor Show. By 1971 M/Benz had approved the conversions, dealers were also approved and took four cars a month, with a total of over 400 being sold.

V8 M/Benz (116) conversions to Estate Cars launched.

## Part III

**1970** – Austin 3 Litre Estate launched. Like most Crayford Estates it had some roof panel work done at FLM in Fulham. At £595 + Car. sales were tiny.

**1971** – David McMullan set up another overseas Crayford operation, this time in South Africa with Cooper and Cooper in Johannesburg, building 114 estates for wealthy farmers, and also launching the Polecat Amphibian ATV in South Africa.

**1972** – Crayford imported from Italy the Lawril Microcar, marketing it as The William Microcar, the worlds smallest 4 wheel car at 80 inches. Only 5 were imported: the first arrived damaged, the rest were hard to sell. Also imported from Italy was the Di Blasi 50cc folding motorcycle in a bag, which fitted inside a car boot, or on a boat deck. These were a big success and Crayford marketed hundreds over the next 10 years, as the Crayford Puma Packaway.

Crayford launched the Mk.3 Cortina Sunshine conversion. Like the Mk.2 it had a long run and sold over 400 units, mainly through Crayford's link with Bristol Street Motors and Phillips Motors (known as The Convertible Car Centre) at Chalk Farm, near Regents Park in London.

*A William Microcar at Westerham*

**1973** – Crayford Litzenfabrication was set up in Germany / Belgium to build under Licence both Mini and Ford Taunus (German Cortina) convertibles.

**1974** – Crayford launched the Westerham built, all new M/Benz 'S' as an Estate Car. Very expensive, around 15 sold, including one for Sophia Lorean to carry her 5 dogs, as a direct order from M/Benz. The car was also sold to rich clients in the USA where it was built locally for Crayford by Hooper's of Detroit. The 'S' class Crayford won Specialist Class gold medal at Barcelona Motor Show.

**1975** – Crayford Allegro launched in Spain at The Barcelona Motor Show. By now Spain was Crayford's biggest export market. Spikin's of Twickenham paid development costs, but only 19 were sold, as BMC car had too weak a bodyshell. Even concrete sills were considered; most shells had leaks and quality control problems. Crayford pulled the plug and refused to make any more.

BL 2200 series 5 door Hatchback launched by Crayford and was so successful that British Leyland corrected their mistake with a factory 5 door car. The 2200 range is re-launched as the Princess range of models, with tailgate.

**1976 –** Crayford went upmarket with the launch of an Audi 100 Cabriolet with expensive hood that includes fixed glass. This and increased volumes of M/Benz conversions marked the beginning of the end of an era with BMC products. On March 1st, Audi 100 Estate added to Crayford line-up. Conversion cost £2,040.

**1978 –** Crayford launched the exclusive and very expensive, (over £10,000 ) conversion of the New W123 M/Benz 280C into a convertible, with a power-operated hood. It was called the Crayford 'St.Tropez' cabriolet.

## Part IV

**1978 –** Crayford's last BL product the TR7 'Tracer' Sports Estate was developed for Triumph dealer, Page Motors of Epsom, as a design exercise. The three door TR7 failed to get a single order at the Motor show despite huge interest. The show car became a one off. Later Volvo produced a copycat, the Volvo 240 ES.

Upmarket Crayford Cortina Mk.4 launched. Cars could be sold by Bristol Street Motors as new cars with full warranties. This was achieved with use of a full roll cage within a padded T-top, similar to the Triumph Stag.

Crayford launched similar Vauxhall 'Centaur' based on the new Cavalier/Manta. It later had full UK type approval. Magraw Eng Ltd built 118, all numbered, under licence to

Crayford .Car cost £7,103, of which £2,808 was for the conversion. As a full size 5 seater convertible it had little competition.

**1980** – The Crayford 'Condor' a one off style exercise for a three door M/Benz 450 SLC sportswagen was exhibited and sold at the NEC Motor Show. So too, was a VW Sirocco Crayford convertible with a power operated hood. The cars grabbed headlines but the Condor was a one off show car and the Sirocco failed to get a single order, as on the very next stand VW launched the Mk1.Golf GTI Convertible undercutting Crayford by £8,000.The writing was on the wall as all major manufacturers jumped on the convertible revival bandwagon.

The last Convertible Cortina was made for the October Motor Show. Based on the all new Mk.5 Cortina. Crayford had this Mk.5 go through full Ministry of Transport type approval, a world first for a small conversion company. The whole project and the Motor show car, was sold to Carbodies of Coventry, who made and sold over 30 cars. Fully loaded one car cost £14,000 in 1980, as much as a new Jaguar Mk1 XJ6.The Mk.5 Cortina and the Centaur had both cost fortunes to type approve and sales only just recouped these cost.

**1981** – The Fiesta Fly launched and after a short run at Westerham a deal was done with F.English Eng. of Bournmouth. They built a run of approx 30 XR2 convertibles under licence to display at all Ford sport dealers around the country, but at £8,900 in the showroom, they were expensive and slow to sell. Crayford even changed policy and offered the car off the peg, based on a used car, to get the fly convertible below the £3,000 level. Jeff smith designed and built two Austin Metro convertibles alongside David's Fly project. Jeff Smith was shattered that Rappor threatened legal action, claiming the design is theirs. The project was cancelled. ,

**1985** – April 1985 Crayford partner Jeff Smith was killed in a motorcycle accident near Crayford's Spanish villa in Alicante, while out shopping for a gift.

May 1985 the Crayford Owners Club showed AFO 887, Jeff Smith's first car, at the Classic Car show, the day after attending his funeral in Brecon.

Surviving partner David McMullan soldiered on alone for the next two years at Westerham. The mainstay of the business was now the Argocat, an 8 wheel All Terrain Vehicle which replaced the now defunct convertibles. Argo sales were steady at over 30 units a month. Crayford kept a toe in the car conversion world with lucrative one off projects and mild cosmetic specials, such as 'Blue Steel ', an XR3 saloon with a turbo and blue metalflak trick paint. Another was the Crayford Sierra Turbo and the 'Starlight Express', a late Capri 280 again with turbo and trick paint.

## Part V

**1987** – David McMullan decided to retire. The Crayford company whose biggest assets were a worldwide brand label and the ongoing Argo ATV franchise, was sold to a new partnership led by David Butlion, a senior director at GM's Luton factory, truck division. His partner was David Connold. The factory freehold was still owned by David McMullan who leased the premises to the new Crayford owners. The No.3 at Crayford, David's right hand man Eugene Dunn, who apprenticed under Sidney Allard, stayed on under the new management. The Argo made Crayford the world's largest supplier of ATV machines outside North America, and a whole range of three and four wheel ATV bikes was added to their portfolio. David Butlion bought back the M/Benz Condor Sportswagen after it was crashed. He had the unique rear restyled around a GM Cavalier tailgate, the work being outsourced to O'Keefe of Croydon. David Butlion then oversaw the last and biggest Crayford convertible ever, a Leyland International Roadtrain truck, all the work being outsourced including the ragtop, done by Oxted trimming near Westerham.The convertible truck cab was used as starter and pace car in international truck grand-prix racing series all that year.

**1989** – The new Crayford partnership moved the whole Crayford operation to their home territory, Harpenden near Luton, where they already had a Vauxhall main dealership and service operation, and Argo clients in the north and Scotland were closer. During that year David Connold bought out David Butlion to become sole owner of Crayford.

He took the company into the JCB Group and moved the whole operation again, this time to the JCB HQ at Hemel Hempstead. He had money in the JCB Group and the Argo fitted well into their line up.

**1990–3** – Alan Brooks joined the company as 25% shareholder and in 1992 David Connold sold his shares to Alan's friends and new business partners who owned one of the largest JCB Dealerships in the country. In 1993 the Crayford Group moved to their premises in Hemel Hempstead.

**1996** – After a short one year lease to Overload Electronics, the historic Westerham factory was empty and soon fell into dis-repair, David McMullan still owns the freehold, but is now retired in Spain. Working part time as an Oxfam engineer in worldwide hotspots. David sold the freehold to a local developer and in June 1996 in only one day, the historic landmark that was Britain's last independent conversion company for four decades, ended when the site was levelled to make way for a small housing estate, even the cottage that had been the office block, and thought to be listed, (like much of Westerham village), was reduced to a pile of rubble.

**1999** – The Crayford Group purchased and moved into their own premises in St.Albans. They are still Distributors of the Argo range of ATV's, plus quad and tri ATV bikes, and now also market small 2 man hovercraft, selling the first two to BAA, Heathrow as rescue craft. They also market RIB Catamarans manufactured in South Africa, by a company bought by David Butlion who moved back to Cape Town in 1993.

**1999** – David McMullan's son Sean who worked at the Westerham factory for his father had started up his own company, Crayford Coachworks L.A in California. He was joined shortly afterwards by his brother Peter.

**2000** – Alan Brooks purchased all of the shares of the Crayford Group to become 100% owner.

**2005** – David Butlion sadly died from cancer and Crayford L.A closed in USA

**2010** – Alastair Brooks, Alan's son, became Managing Director of Argo Vehicles Limited, a new company which was set up to take over the vehicle trading arm of Crayford and the Argo franchise. Alan semi-retired to take a back seat, although he still retains ownership of the premises and other companies within the Crayford Group.

**2012** – Crayford still thrive as a company specialising in all-terrain vehicles, off-road 3-wheeler bikes, hovercraft, and have a boat division in Scotland. Today they are based in St Albans off the M25, north of London. Crayford LA did not make a new conversion before they closed, but did redesign the Porsche Boxter chassis for many Californian owners to take hard, mountain driving without fracturing the original chassis.

Financially successful, they folded when the land under and around them was sold for a corporate luxury development.

# Bits and Bobs

## Part I

**1975** Mumford paid Crayford £3,849 for the licence to build the Crayford Marina Convertible

**1974** Cooper & Cooper of Johannesburg, South Africa, paid Crayford 1800 Rand for five years to build the Crayford M/Benz estates, producing a brochure in Afrikaans.

A 'CRAYFORD' Motor Show stand banner at Earls Court cost £34.34

Crayford quoted £4,480 + VAT to convert a Rolls Royce Silver Shadow into an Estate Car.

In November, Spikins of Twickenham, a BL main dealer, paid the last of three instalments to Crayford for developing the Allegro convertible. In all they paid Crayford £4,536 for the complete project. The car is launched at Barcelona Motor Show.

Crayford pulled the plug on the convertible Allegro, after only approx 17 cars, as the shell was found to be too weak for the conversion, it was not possible to eliminate very bad scuttle shake in the car. Even concrete poured into the sills failed. One unregistered car sent for conversion, had a bent wheel, and toe in out of alignment by 5/32. Crayford also found broken glass under the carpets, serious steering and geometry faults, plus extensive evidence of repair and respray, all on a supposedly new car. It had been crashed but they said it was none of our business if some poor sap bought it as a new car.

In August Crayford shipped to Mr Godison of 115 Bell Road, St lucia, Brisbane in Queensland, Australia, a R.H.D Porsche 914, it was registered QP 1706. It must have been a very rare car in Aussie, even then. The left to right hand drive conversion on the Porsche was a big seller in the U.K too. Crayford also had an enquiry for the conversion from HRH The crown Prince of Jahore in Malaysia.

**1977** Harpers of Detroit, Michigan paid Crayford a £10,400 Licence fee to build the M/Benz 116 'S' class estate in America.

Sargent & Collins the Crayford dealer for the Mercedes Estate conversions on the 114 had sold 74 cars from its small Sussex dealership in one year alone.

**1975** (Dec) Leyland did send a white Triumph stag (1974 spec) to Crayford for evaluation and as a base car for conversion to a prototype stag Estate. Leyland also looked at Crayford's artwork for the Stag Estate. All Leyland's letters on the project referred to the car as 'The Staghound'. The project never progressed any further, no Stag estate was built in any form, Crayford were appalled at its build quality.

**1978** The TR7 Estate project from week ending 2-12-1977 to 22-06-1978 costed out at 629 manhours, and 15 minutes. A total of £1,889-75p in wages alone.

## Part II

In the **1960**s Crayford took part in a Trade Delegation to the USA: one aim was to see if there was a market in America for the Crayford Cortina Mk2 convertible. But Ford UK had just had a campaign to sell the Cortina Mk2 saloon range to the American market as a cheap compact. They had a spares and servicing facility (nightmare!), trying to cover all America on a small budget. The Cortina saloon was also dearer and had less spec. then the home-grown Ford (USA) Pinto. Despite showing a convertible Cortina Mk2 at the Chicago Motor show, Crayford – like Ford – decided the cars could not be exported and make good profits. It was a non-starter.

In 1969 (March) Crayford used well-known tuning company V. W. Derrington to supply 9 sets of hand made exhausts for a batch of 3-Litre V6 Mk.2 Crayford Cortinas to be shipped out to Spain on 27th March.

**1972** (June) Crayford started work for A.M.C Motors of Chiswick, in west London. Crayford were contracted to convert from left- to righthand drive, all the AMC Ambassador models imported to the UK from AMC (USA). Most were black cars, issued to embassy and military staff working in London. The total conversion cost AMC £330 inc VAT. After development by Crayford, the work was farmed out to Mumford, who also built Marina convertibles. A total of 31 AMC cars were converted up to September 1973.

**1973** (October), Britain had record new car sales, and a scorching summer. But the convertible market had collapsed, so, too, the demand for Crayford's as winter approached. Bristol Street Motors agreed to Crayford's demands to order two Crayford Cortina's every month for the next year, rather then risk Crayford cancelling the Mk.4 convertible programme. It guaranteed work at Westerham all through the winter and into 1974.

Crayford used a gentleman called J. J. Lambert from Sanderstead, Surrey, to produce artwork to show prospective Crayford clients how their conversions would look. He charged

£15 to produce a pen and ink drawing. His work included Range Rover, Allegro, Mercedes Benz and interestingly, 'Avenger Convertible'.

**1977** (May) Crayford began the Centaur project for Magraw Engineering Ltd to build a Vauxhall Cavalier T Top convertible. Crayford charged a fee £12,100 to start the project. And £5,800 to produce the first prototype Centaur with drop-down rear qtr glass, which did not make it to the 118 cars produced. It cost £6,300 to take the car through full approval by the Ministry of Transport. In November 1977 the first production Centaur is allocated the number 025, the next 026 and so on. It was often thought they were numbered from 001 to 118, but many manufacturers do not for some reason start from 001

For the 1977 Motor Show Crayford produced a German Ford Taunus version of their successful Mk.4 Cortina convertible, priced at £4,700 This 1.6 litre LHD car was sold after the show to Albion S. A in Madrid, Spain, for £4,000.

## Part III

In **1971** a normal BMC 1800 Landcrab conversion into a five door hatchback would cost you £214.It was one of Crayford's longest running conversions (12 years ) and very profitable. The Road Research Laboratory ordered two very special 1800 landcrab Estates from Crayford. These had revised bodywork, full length platforms on the roof and ladders on the rear wing, to reach the roof. They where use as mobile filming platforms for early crash testing research .Two were delivered in November at a whopping conversion cost of £954 each.

In 1973 work started in November on a Crayford Cortina 2000 GT for MP and member of the House of Lords, Lord Morris of Kenwood, who lived in Kingston, Surrey. He took

Crayford's 'GTS 125 ' package, a 125 BHP engine, with new tuned heads and carbsV6 engine, coachline's, new wheels and a cloth upgrade for the hood instead of standard PVC. There was also a bonnet scoop.

In 1973 in May director David McMullan wrote a report after his recent visit to South Africa to visit Cooper & Cooper in Johannesburg, who where building the Crayford Mercedes Estates locally under licence. David reported he saw little of interest to him on the continent, except a beautifully engineered Ford Granada with a 5 Litre V8 conversion. David also observed the huge popularity of the saloon based pick up truck, a trend not taken up in Europe. He rightly deduced the reason was that they, the white bosses, did not have to travel with their black workers. A common site on long road trips were these Cortina pickups with one white boss in the car and up to twenty black workers hanging on for dear life in the back and on the cab roof. It was all another part of apartied. Time would eventually change all this.

In 1973 Crayford ship by air to Ford dealer Viipurin Autola Oy in Kouvola, Finland, one complete crayford Cortina conversion kit, for local assembly.

In **1975** at the Motor Show at Earls Court, Crayford were approached by Alfa Romeo (GB) Ltd, to try their new Alfetta in the Show's press fleet to evaluate the possibility of producing a Alfetta Sportswagen estate. Crayford took a close look at the car and estimated it would add £2,100 to the cost of an Alfetta saloon, and around £8/9000 to develop the first prototype Crayford Alfa Alfetta Estate. It was not pursued by Alfa UK when news filtered through that the new Alfasud, planned by the factory in Italy, was to have a sporstswagen in its future range.

*Ford Capri Exterminator*

*Audio 100 Cabriolet*

# Crayford Conversions

***Convertibles***

BMC Mini
BMC Mini Cooper
BMC 1300
BMC Allegro
BMC Marina
BMC Wolseley Hornet (Heinz 57)
BMC Austin 3 litre
AUSTIN Metro (Metropolitan)
FORD Cortina MK.1
FORD Cortina MK.2
FORD Cortina MK.2 Cabriolet
FORD Cortina MK.3
FORD Cortina MK.4
FORD Cortina MK.5
FORD Corsair
FORD Corsair Cabriolet
FORD Capri (Caprice)
FORD Fiesta (Fly)
FORD Fiesta MK.2
FORD Lotus Cortina MK.1
FORD Lotus Cortina MK.2
FORD Escord MK.1

FORD Escort MK.2
M/BENZ 280CE Cabriolet (St.Tropez)
AUDI 100 Cabriolet
OPAL Commodore
OPAL Manta (Centaur)
VAUXHALL Viva HB Cabriolet
VAUXHALL Cavalier (Centaur)
VW SIRROCO (Tempest)
WILLIAM – MICROCAR
BMW 1602 Cabriolet

***All-terrain vehicles***
HILLFARMER (8 wheel)
AMPHICAT (6 wheel)
POLECAT (4 wheel)
ARGOCAT (6-8-16-20 wheel)
PUMA 50cc ‘MOTORBIKE-IN-A-BAG

***Estates***
BMC 1100/1300
BMC 1800/2200
LEYLAND Princess
TRIUMPH TR7 (Tracer)
AUDI 100
M-BENZ ‘S’ Class(/8 )
M-BENZ ‘S’ Class V8 (116)
M-BENZ 114
ROVER P6 (FLM)
TORCAR Marina Camper

***Saloon Engine Swaps***
FORD Cortina MK.2 V6 3LTR
FORD Capri MK.3 Turbo
FORD Capri MK.1 V8
ESCORT MK.1 V6 (Eliminator)
FORD Sierra Turbo

BMW 2800 / 3ltre APINA
BMW 2002 Turbo

***One-offs***
MINI Carnival Beach Car
M-BENZ 230 EST. stretched
M-BENZ 450 SLC EST(Condor)
M-BENZ 350 SEL Laundette
M-BENZ 600 Laundette
FORD Fiesta Amphibian
D/Telegraph MK.2 Camper
Leyland RoadTrain Truck

***Left to righthand conversions***
AMC Rambler Ambassaor
PORSCHE 914 / 916

*Jeff Smith, always a powerful and determined rider, prepared his machines with his motto that ran through Crayford: "near enough is not good enough".*

*Jeff Smith racing the works' Lambretta sidecar outfit. The passenger, David McMullan, was thrown out into the crowd at the next bend.*

*David Mc Mullan driving his Cooper at Brands Hatch 1959*

*David McMullan briefs King Hussein of Jordan in 1960 before a test drive in a racing kart. Thirty years later he radioed the King for help when stranded on the Iraq–Jordanian frontier during the war.*

*Sean and Peter in California, May 2011*

*A rare moment: 2 Crayford S Class Mercedes Estates outside the Los Angeles Crayford premises with Sean and Peter McMullan.*

*Three Crayford Corsair convertibles were on display in the 2012 London Olympics closing ceremony as part of the demonstration of British engineering style and flair.*

*A Corsair (front right) under wraps*

*Celebrating sixty years of competitive motorcycling:*
*David McMullan in the Torrequemada, Denia, Spain, 2012.*
*Photograph courtesy of Román Rodríguez*